EN EL SECADERO DE ALMAS
poesía cubana de la generación cero

IN THE DRYING SHED OF SOULS
poetry from cuba's generation zero

with selections from

Luis Yuseff, Isaily Pérez González, Javier Marimón Miyares,
Leymen Pérez García, Marcelo Morales Cintero, Óscar Cruz,
Liuvan Herrera Carpio, Jamila Medina Ríos, Moisés Mayán
Fernández, Legna Rodríguez Iglesias & Sergio García Zamora

introduced, selected, and translated by

Katherine M. Hedeen & Víctor Rodríguez Núñez

the operating system
GLOSSARIUM : UNSILENCED TEXTS
print//document

EN EL SECADERO DE ALMAS : Poesía cubana de la Generación Cero
IN THE DRYING SHED OF SOULS: Poetry from Cuba's Generation Zero

ISBN: 978-1-946031-48-8
Library of Congress CIP Number: 2019902611
copyright © 2019 by Luis Yuseff, Isaily Pérez González, Javier Marimón Miyares, Leymen Pérez García, Marcelo Morales Cintero, Óscar Cruz, Liuvan Herrera Carpio, Jamila Medina Ríos, Moi Mayán Fernández, Legna Rodríguez Iglesias, Sergio García Zamora

translation copyright © 2019 by Katherine M. Hedeen and Víctor Rodríguez Núñez
edited and designed by ELÆ [Lynne DeSilva-Johnson]
additional interior design: Zoe Guttenplan

is released under a Creative Commons CC-BY-NC-ND (Attribution, Non Commercial, Derivatives) License: its reproduction is encouraged for those who otherwise could not afford purchase in the case of academic, personal, and other creative usage from which no profit will accr Complete rules and restrictions are available at:
http://creativecommons.org/licenses/by-nc-nd/3.0/

For additional questions regarding reproduction, quotation, or to request a pdf for review contact operator@theoperatingsystem.org

This text was set in Caslon, Vinyl, Brisk, Abuget, and OCR-A Std.

Cover art uses: *El vuelo* (Estudio para una ilustración publicada en El Caimán Barbudo) / The Flight (Study for an Illustration Published in El Caimán Barbudo), 1982. India ink / paper, 37.5 cm x 51 cm, by Tonel. Artist's Collection. (Provided by / used with permission of the artist.) [Image description: black and white ink illustration of a human head in profile with a tongue flying out of its mouth.]

Your donation makes our publications, platform and programs possible! We <3 You.
http://theoperatingsystem.org/subscribe-join/

the operating system
www.theoperatingsystem.org
operator@theoperatingsystem.org

EN EL SECADERO DE ALMAS
poesía cubana de la generación cero

IN THE DRYING SHED OF SOULS
poetry from cuba's generation zero

GLOSSARIUM : UNSILENCED TEXTS
the operating system c. 2019

2019 OS SYSTEM OPERATORS

CREATIVE DIRECTOR/FOUNDER/MANAGING EDITOR: ELÆ
[Lynne DeSilva-Johnson]

DEPUTY EDITOR: Peter Milne Greiner
CONTRIBUTING EDITOR, EX-SPEC-PO: Kenning JP Garcia
CONTRIBUTING EDITOR, FIELD NOTES: Adrian Silbernagel
CONTRIBUTING EDITOR, IN CORPORE SANO: Amanda Glassman
CONTRIBUTING EDITOR, GLOSSARIUM: Ashkan Eslami Fard
CONTRIBUTING ED. GLOSSARIUM / RESOURCE COORDINATOR:
Bahaar Ahsan
JOURNEYHUMAN / SYSTEMS APPRENTICE: Anna Winham
DIGITAL CHAPBOOKS / POETRY MONTH COORDINATOR: Robert Balun
TYPOGRAPHY WRANGLER / DEVELOPMENT COORDINATOR: Zoe Guttenplan
DESIGN ASSISTANTS: Lori Anderson Moseman, Orchid Tierney, Michael Flatt
SOCIAL SYSTEMS / HEALING TECH: Curtis Emery
VOLUNTEERS and/or ADVISORS: Adra Raine, Alexis Quinlan, Clarinda Mac Low, Bill Considine, Careen Shannon, Joanna C. Valente, L. Ann Wheeler, Erick Sáenz, Knar Gavin, Joe Cosmo Cogen, Charlie Stern, Audrey Gascho, Michel Bauwens, Christopher Woodrell, Liz Maxwell, Margaret Rhee, Lydia X. Y. Brown, Lauren Blodgett, Semir Chouabi, J. Lester Feder, Margaretha Haughwout, Alexandra Juhasz, Caits Meissner, Mehdi Navid, Hoa Nguyen, Margaret Randall, Benjamin Wiessner

The Operating System is a member of the **Radical Open Access Collective**, a community of scholar-led, not-for-profit presses, journals and other open access projects. Now consisting of 40 members, we promote a progressive vision for open publishing in the humanities and social sciences.

Learn more at: http://radicaloa.disruptivemedia.org.uk/about/

Your donation makes our publications, platform and programs possible! We <3 You.
http://www.theoperatingsystem.org/subscribe-join/

CONTENTS

Introduction	7
Luis Yuseff (Holguín, 1975)	13
Isaily Pérez González (Santa Clara, 1975)	29
Javier Marimón Miyares (Matanzas, 1975)	41
Leymen Pérez García (Matanzas, 1976)	51
Marcelo Morales Cintero (Havana, 1977)	65
Óscar Cruz (Santiago de Cuba, 1979)	79
Liuvan Herrera Carpio (Fomento, 1981)	95
Jamila Medina Ríos (Holguín, 1981)	109
Moisés Mayán Fernández (Holguín, 1983)	123
Legna Rodríguez Iglesias (Camagüey, 1984)	135
Sergio García Zamora (Esperanza, 1986)	149

INTRODUCTION

In a recent interview, the renowned Polish poet, Adam Zagajewski, declared that in his country, "poetry killed communism." We don't bring this up to question his position and experience. We are more interested in calling attention to the fact that the situation of Cuban poets is actually quite different from that of those poets who lived through Europe's "real socialism." In other words, thinking in terms of dissident intellectual versus official intellectual doesn't really work in the case of Cuba, where most poets want to escape such a reductive binary and, ultimately, be independent.

It's not a cliché by any means to declare that few times in its history has Cuban poetry been more varied, innovative, critical, and attractive than it is right now. And an undeniable part of it is what has been written by the so-called Generation Zero (Generación Cero), poets born after 1970 and who begin publishing after 2000. It's a numerous group, as the title of their most complete anthology illustrates, *La isla en versos: Cien poetas cubanos* [The Island in Verse: One Hundred Cuban poets] (2011 and 2013). In fact, our selection was compiled having read over sixty books, tens of anthologies, and numerous journals and magazines. Indeed, the only way to truly do justice to this poetry is to offer up book-length anthologies; our aim in these pages is to be the first to simply introduce it to English-speaking readers.

Elsewhere we've defended the notion that Cuban poetry was revolutionary before the Revolution. It continued to be in the midst of profound transformations that took place on the island beginning in 1959, despite revolutionary power's paradoxical mistrust of it. It still is after the Revolution's decline, which arose in the nineties. It's revolutionary not because it's neo-romantic, neo-realist (much less socialist-realist), colloquial, or neo-baroque; but because it renounces solipsism, the differentiation of the other, and it does so in diverse ways, with notable creative freedom.

Generation Zero is no exception. The work presented here reaffirms Cuba's long, rich tradition of dialogic poetry, which finds its identity through the identification with the other, and is marked by tensions between commitment and autonomy, dialogue and creativity, continuity and rupture. It is poetry with vast experience in the representations of subordinations (nation, class, gender, ethnicity, sexuality) in order to subvert them, that has consciously participated in both social and cultural transformations, that has drawn closer to popular language and culture, and that has decolonized itself in content and in form.

This brilliance has shown through in the midst of the dismal social situation that has crisscrossed the island since the start of the nineties. The fall of European socialism meant Cuba lost 85 percent of its trade, sparking the deepest economic crisis in its history. Daily life became hell: lines, rationing, hunger, panhandling, prostitution, crime. The solution for many Cubans was summed up in two verbs: *resolver* and *inventar* (roughly translated as "getting by any way you can"), without necessarily respecting any ethical principle. Hundreds of thousands emigrated to the United States or wherever they could.

Generation Zero was forced to grow up under these kind of circumstances, with no opportunities or future. And its poetry embodies the crisis in countless ways, directly or indirectly. Like in Oscar Cruz's work, it focuses on new social marginality with severity, but also tenderness. It offers us its poetic antihero, its difficult relationship with community, its acknowledgement of life and writing as a struggle. This critical view of reality is, as Isaily Pérez González, Leymen Pérez García, Moisés Mayán Fernández, and Liuvan Herrera Carpio reveal, sometimes hopeless, and yet always based on an identification with the other.

The themes here are also pensive, with notable intellectual depth. Like in the case of Marcelo Morales Cintero, poetic writing becomes fundamentally thought. Not philosophy, not ethics, not politics, but interaction between reason and feeling. In this interpellation of reality, at all its levels, edges blur, categories like objective and subjective, private and public, stop making sense. What binds the poetic subject to the other, to otherness, is love, transcending family or sex.

Another constant is the ambivalent positioning before both cultural and political tradition. On the one hand, Luis Yussef's lyrical hero is positive, identifies politically, but in cultural terms. His understanding of geography and history goes far beyond national borders, but the universal can show up in a local coffeehouse, become part of bitter daily life. On the other, as in the case of Legna Rodríguez Iglesias, there's a negative discourse of difference, unafraid of being openly political.

A major standout of this poetry is the way it represents the feminine condition. In this regard, Jamila Medina Ríos' work offers a soaring level of poetic elaboration. There are no inhibitions here, moving beyond traditional feminism and timeworn lists of women's body parts, to give voice to sexualities that challenge the norm. With indisputable grace and personality, Rodríguez Iglesias' poetry takes all this on as well, reluctant to make one single concession, with pleasure and suffering to the very end. González Pérez's poetry challenges too, but in its own way, with a more subtle exploration of the difficulties of Cuban reality experienced through the lens of gender.

Themes intertwine, appear and later disappear, like in our own minds, our own lives. Ultimately, this poetry expresses a critical consciousness, growing from childhood roots, not forgetting to be self-critical or limited to the personal. In this way, it challenges every ideology, whether it be idealist or materialist, rightist or leftist. What comes to the fore is a rejection of solipsism and an affirmation of the invention of reality, a dialogue unwilling to sell out to populism or the market, and the need for a participative reader.

This thematic boldness, never seen before in Cuban poetry, is complemented by no less daring work with language. In what seems to be a generational trademark, Sergio García Zamora alternates between prose poems, –since they lend themselves well to reflection–, and neo-Avant-Garde verse poems, because of the intentional distribution of the text on the page, and the abandoning of upper-case letters and punctuation. Pérez García, Morales Cintero, Herrera Carpio, Medina Ríos and Rodríguez Iglesias do the same. There is a search for another mode of expression, just like with all self-respecting poetry.

Indeed, here there is a wide range of styles. While Yussef uses an expanding verse, capable of representing different planes of reality at once, Javier Marimón Miyares opts for a synthetic, neo-baroque verse where the hyperbaton rules. And while for Morales Cintero the poem stops being a unit of poetic writing, giving up that place to the book, and verse draws carefully, elegantly closer to prose, in Cruz what prevails is a poetry that moves toward the colloquial and song. In each case, language is refined, cultured and at the same time popular, and the rhythm that distinguishes it as poetry is preserved.

Still, these days, no one expects this kind of poetry from a Cuban, not in literary circles in the Spanish-speaking world, on the left or the right, not in North American academic and creative writing circles either. And perhaps that's why it hasn't received the attention it deserves.

For the former, it's because the poetry isn't communicative, and instead welcomes an active reader who participates in the creation of meaning. Cuban poetry has had to confront, above all in the seventies, neo-Stalinist aesthetic standards, which demanded, among other things, "reaching the people," being clear and direct. This is precisely one of the paradigms of the so-called "poetry of experience," which prevails in Spain today, with offshoots in Latin America, especially among the contemporaries of Generation Zero, the self-designated "poets of uncertainty." By contrast, the young poets selected here are very well aware, from historical experience, of the danger of making aesthetic concessions in the name of coherence and transparency, and, as such, they defend poetry's integrity.

For the latter, it's because the poetry isn't exotic enough, doesn't explicitly focus on the difficult material and spiritual situation Cuba has lived through ever since the fall of European socialism and the disintegration of the USSR. Contemporary Cuban poetry isn't subject to the market like narrative is, and so it's not forced to speak of opportunistic bureaucrats, prostitutes with college degrees, blackouts and endless lines, the splendor of the black market. Indeed, the crisis experienced on the island is well-represented in these pages, but without making any concessions to exoticism. There's a critical perspective, a profound uneasiness, but no absolute opposition, no automatic negation. Instead, the negation of the negation is what comes to the fore, the need for a social alternative, but not anticommunism, not a call for the return of capitalism.

The most notable exclusion of these poets appears in the anthology *El canon abierto: Última poesía en español* [The Open Canon: New Poetry in Spanish] edited by Remedios Sánchez García, selected by Anthony L. Geist, and published by Visor, the most prestigious poetry press in Spain, in 2015. The back cover reads, "nearly two hundred researchers from more than one hundred universities (Harvard, Oxford, Columbia, and Princeton, among them) have chosen the most relevant poets in the Spanish language born after 1970." Among the forty selected, not one is from Cuba; in fact, in the "Full List of Cited Poets," which includes one hundred twenty-two authors, just one Cuban is mentioned.

Yet, though they are relatively isolated, whether it be because of extremely limited access to the Internet or the difficulties of traveling off the island, these poets aren't behind the times at all, on the contrary, they are at the forefront of poetry being written anywhere in the world. Here there's no trace of superficiality, no fear of emotional complexity or intellectual density, of formal rigor or experimentation. It's poetry open to reality and the most diverse forms of representation. The authors know that intellectuals participate in society through their cultural production.

In short, the critique these poets make of present day Cuban society and culture not only transcends the Cuban government's version of the facts but also platitudes about anticommunism, making such a critique more profound. It's possible because it carries with it an understanding of poetry's essential function as a counter-ideology. If all ideologies base their discourse on making the artificial seem natural, poetry denaturalizes our perception of the world; it considers everything as if it were for the first time. This it where poetry derives its political force from, just as it does its explicit or implicit challenging of power, its ability to change life.

Luis Yuseff (Holguín 1975) is a poet and editor. He is the author of eleven books of prize-winning poetry, the latest being *Dolor de resurrección* (2014), which received the prestigious Gaceta de Cuba Poetry Prize. Two editions of his Selected Poems have appeared on the island. He has also selected and edited two anthologies, one of Cuban poets and another of Cuban prose writers. He lives in Holguín.

Esquema de la impura rosa

a Joaquín Osorio

I

Contra las Montañas Rocosas de Colorado estaba el Viajero del Paleolítico, de perfil eternamente detenido, silbando *La vida en rosa*, apenas silbando/ rumiando *La vida en rosa* (¿O era la *Barcarola* de *Los cuentos de Hoffmann*?). Dios no había inventado aún las palabras con que 32 millones de años después habrían de nombrarlo Olofi, Jehová o Padre Zeus. Ni tampoco había creado al hombre, pero ya estaba el Viajero desde entonces contra las Montañas Rocosas de Colorado, silbando *La vida en rosa*. Deshojando la mítica centifolia sin saber que la rosa es un abismo que miente.

II

Que miente.
La rosa es un abismo que miente sobre la mesa de musicar tristezas.
Y Violeta Parra, la indiecita andina de París, está interrogando a la rosa mapuche que, de espalda a la marcialidad de los veranos y doblándose despacio

*(tan despacio que mata
palomito volador, me quieres?)*

le responde. Pero no hay que creerle.
La rosa es un abismo que miente. Y Violeta es frágil como un segundo. Fugaz, con las manos ásperas de sacarle música a la pobreza, dibuja sobre el barro dos cuerpos niños.
Después sopla, mientras en las noches de nunca acabar, con los dientes callándose el hambre, tiritando, teje y desteje a merced de la inspiración.
Ángel e Isabel, como dos violincitos asustados, protestan en pizzicato, duermen en el estuche de la guitarra columpiándose desde lo más alto de la Carpa de la Reina.
"Mientras no se te venga encima Violeta mía -le ha dicho el viajero. Mientras te dure el espectáculo. Vamos, todavía le quedan 3 pétalos a tu rosa. Y deshojar una rosa es como preguntarle a Dios..."

¿Palomito volador, me quieres?

Blueprint of an Impure Rose

to Joaquín Osorio

I

Up against the Rocky Mountains in Colorado was the Paleolithic Traveler, in profile eternally prisoner, whistling "La Vie en Rose," scarcely whistling/ humming "La Vie en Rose" (or was it the Barcarolle from *The Tales of Hoffman*?). God hadn't even made up the words 32 million years later Olofi, Jehovah, or Father Zeus would use to name him. He hadn't created man yet either, still the Traveler was there up against the Rocky Mountains in Colorado, whistling "La vie en rose." Pulling the petals off the mythical centifolia not knowing the rose is a lying abyss.

II

Lying.
The rose is a lying abyss on the table of sorrows set to music.
And Violeta Parra, the Andean Indian from Paris, is questioning the Mapuche rose, back turned to the martiality of summers and slowly bending over

(*so slowly it kills
sweet flying dove, do you love me?*)

it answers. But we don't have to believe it.
The rose is a lying abyss. And Violeta is fragile like a second. Fleeting, hands rough from mining music out of poverty, she draws two children's bodies on the clay.
Later she blows, while on never-ending nights, with teeth quieting hunger, trembling, she weaves and unweaves at inspiration's mercy.
Ángel and Isabel, like two tiny frightened violins, protest in pizzicato, asleep in the guitar case, swinging from the highest point of the Carpa de la Reina LP.
"As long as it doesn't all come crashing down on you my Violeta," the traveler told her. "As long as the show lasts. Come on, your rose still has 3 petals. And pulling the petals off a rose is like asking God..."

Sweet flying dove, do you love me?

Y la rosa interrogada le responde.
En la Candelaria.
En un rinconcito húmedo de París.
En la *rue* Monsieur le Prince No.3.

III

Y en el 3 concurren otras 2 rosas: la solícita Cagí, y la no menos solícita Rosa la China, asegurando por puro instinto -como los grandes sabios- que aún antes de Cristo hubo rosas. Que del Asia le vienen todas las rosas a este mundo. Y que este mundo sin rosas no sería este mundo sino la tristeza de Sandro di Mariano di Vanni Filipepi Botticelli, sin un pétalo siquiera para acompañar el nacimiento de Venus. O la tristeza de Yukio Mishima, frente al San Sebastián de Guido Reni, con la rosa de la masturbación entre los puños ofreciendo sus fluidos seminales. El licor áspero y amargo del suicidio.

IV

Qué sería de este mundo sin la rosa... Le preguntas a la rosa.
Y la rosa te responde: Qué sería de la rosa sin la rosa...
Qué hubiera sido del Adelantado Don Cristóbal, si una sola de las rosas de los cuatro vientos se hubiera ausentado en el instante en que Rodrigo de Triana, desde lo más alto de las tres carabelas y chillando como ave de palo, le anuncia al Nuevo Mundo la llegada del mismísimo Dios de Doña Isabel y Don Fernando.
Qué sería de este mundo sin la rosa.
Qué de Julieta o más bien qué de Romeo.
Qué del Cisne de Avon y del ruiseñor. Y de la rosa.
Qué sería de la rosa sin la rosa.

V

Y qué de Nerón y sus 150 mil secretas noches de placer.
Qué del Palacio Dorado y la Palatina, sino el deseo flotando bocarriba en las copas de vino como una rosa.
Y ni pensar qué hubiera sido de la bella Cleopatra, pues al pecho enamorado de Marco Antonio se llega por un camino de rosas.
Y qué de Hera, Afrodita y Atenea, frente a la sabia Eris, trocando rosas por manzanas.
Dejando caer a los ojos de la divina vanidad la rosa de la discordia.

And the questioned rose answers.
In the Candelaria.
In a damp corner of Paris.
On the rue Monsieur le Prince Number 3.

III

And at Number 3 come together another 2 roses: the solicitous Rosa Cagí and the no less solicitous Rosa la China, promising out of pure instinct –like great wise men– that there were roses even before Christ. That all the roses in this world came from Asia. And this roseless world wouldn't be this world without the sadness of Sandro di Mariano di Vanni Filipepi Botticelli, without even one petal to keep the birth of Venus company. Or the sadness of Yukio Mishima, facing Guido Reni's "Saint Sebastian," with the rose of masturbation between fists, offering up seminal fluids. The suicide's rough, absinthian liquor.

IV

What would this world be without the rose... You ask the rose.
And the rose answers: What would the rose be without the rose...
What would the Adelantado Don Christopher have been, if only one of the roses of the four winds had disappeared at the moment when Rodrigo de Triana, screeching like a wooden bird from the top of the three caravels, proclaimed to the New World the arrival of the very same God as Doña Isabella's and Don Ferdinand's.
What would this world be without the rose.
What of Juliet or what of Romeo rather.
What of the Bard of Avon and the nightingale. And the rose.
What would the rose be without the rose.

V

And what of Nero and his 150 thousand secret nights of pleasure.
What of the Golden Palace and the Palatine Chapel, but desire floating face-up in glasses of wine like a rose.
And impossible to think what would have been of the beautiful Cleopatra, for a path of roses leads to Marc Antony's smitten heart.
And what of Hera, Aphrodite and Athena, facing the wise Eris, trading roses for apples.
Letting the rose of discord fall toward the eyes of divine vanity.

Qué sería del Olimpo sin la rosa.

VI

Y si en el reino de Oz no existiera el rosal de Pitiminí.
Qué sería de Shirley Temple.
Y sin la musicalia de la rosa azafranada qué sería de Madrid sin una melodía para alegrar a los Reyes.
Tú sola, Shirley Temple, no podrías alegrar a uno solo de los reyes de este mundo. Tan vastos son en sus celebraciones que hasta para morirse visten bonitos a los caballos.
Tendríamos que buscar cien mil enanos como tú.
Y sembrar el cosmos (la distancia que media entre el infinito y tú, Shirley Temple) de estrellas pequeñitas.
Tan pequeñas como el rosal de Pitiminí.
Por cierto, ahora que ya no estás, dime, Shirley Temple, cómo se las arregla para pasar sin ti el rosal de Pitiminí.

VII

Y la rosa de Bengala. Y la rosa de Pasión, que es una rosa que mata. Y la rosa de Jericó, que es una rosa que miente, crecida en los arenales, simulando muerte para ver el entierro que le hacen, solo para ver el entierro que le hacen, porque una vez que las lloronas palestinas comienzan con sus lamentos la rosita de Jericó abre un pétalo, y otro, y otro pétalo, y se vuelve una envidia de frescura. Lava su inocente picardía en las aguas bautismales del Jordán para ser, otra vez, la rosa de Jericó crecida entre las ruinas.

VIII

Qué sería de los muertos sin la rosa. Le preguntas a la rosa.
Y la rosa te responde *Eternidad*.
Y la Eternidad detiene el último minuto de las Eras Imaginarias frente al Viajero que mira a la mítica centifolia
silbando "La vida en rosa," mascullando "La vida en rosa" (¿O era *La Barcarola* de *Los Cuentos de Hoffmann*?)
mientras se sacude los escombros mortales del pecho contra la ventolera arrasadora de la muerte.

What would Olympus be without the rose.

VI

And what if the miniature rosebush didn't exist in the land of Oz.
What of Shirley Temple.
And without the musicalia of the saffron-scented rose, what of Madrid, no melody to please the King and Queen.
You alone, Shirley Temple, couldn't please even one of the kings of this world. So immense are they in their celebrations that when they die they even dress up horses.
We'd have to find one hundred thousand dwarfs like you.
And sow the cosmos (the distance measured between the infinite and you, Shirley Temple) with tiny little stars.
As tiny as the miniature rosebush.
By the way, now that you're not here, tell me Shirley Temple, how does the miniature rosebush figure out how to get by without you.

VII

And the Bengal rose. And the rose of Passion, which is a murderous rose. And the rose of Jericho, which is a lying rose, grown in sandy spots, faking death to see what kind of a funeral it can get, just to see what kind of funeral it can get, because once the Palestinian mourners begin with their laments the tiny rose of Jericho unfurls a petal, and another, and then another petal, and it turns into the envy of freshness. Washes its innocent mischief in the baptismal waters of the Jordan to be, once more, the rose of Jericho grown in ruins.

VIII

What would the dead be without the rose. You ask the rose.
And the rose answers *Eternity*.
And Eternity imprisons the last minute of the Imaginary Eras before the Traveler looking at the mythical centifolia
whistling "La vie en rose," mumbling "La vie en rose" (or was it the Barcarolle from *The Tales of Hoffman*?)
while he shakes off the mortal rubble from his chest against the raging gusts of death.

Flores de hierro en el pecho de un hombre

Esta noche ha entrado un murciélago a la casa.
Su vuelo es leve, pero torpe.
Advierto: puede ser una maniobra espía.
Pero no oculto entre mis cosas nada que atente contra la seguridad de un pueblo.
Solo trato de escribir unas pocas líneas.
Dos o tres palabras. Versos para hacer música a los oídos de las personas que se invitan a la casa.
Palabras que si algún poder tienen no será el de libertarme.

Poder de libertad.

Así surgen de las sombras estos ojos como la evocación de un fantasma.
Nombres que olvidaré.
Aunque me niegue. Pronto comenzarán a borrarse de mi memoria con el vino ácido de los días.
Con urgencia.
Al frotar fuerte la cabeza contra las paredes.
Al escribir versos a las cambiantes estaciones.
Lejos del trópico. Cosas que han contado los amigos para quedar fuera.
Detrás del enrejado de las almas donde crecen rosas de papel.

Flores de hierro en el pecho de un hombre.

Detrás del enrejado. Trato de iniciar "una vuelta a mi cárcel".
Casa donde los murciélagos se posan y liban sangre en las flores de hierro.
Una vuelta a su cárcel. Los deseos prohibidos de Margarita. El hijo hermoso reventando con su vigor penas sobre la almohada.
Juegos de muerte. Niños como animales disputándose el fruto de la soledad.
Afuera, lejos de los ojos de Ranel, bajo el peso de plomo de sus lunas vencidas, doran los Trípticos en alguna capilla de este mundo donde Dios no se acuerda de él. Ni de Juan, que ha querido ser en los amantes que se alejan. Detenido en los óleos. Con la muerte azul. Compartida.
Escribiendo para escapar del cuerpo.
Armandito, levantándose de hielo en un país de sol. Aquí no se llora.
Se es de terracota a los rezos de la madre espartana.
Por sus venas se vuelve a la isla. Aquí se ama. Y se espera:
Aquí crecen las *flores de hierro: resonantes como el pecho de un hombre.*

Iron Flowers on the Chest of a Man

Tonight a bat's fluttered into the house.
Its flight is easy, but awkward.
Warning: it might be a spy tactic.
Still I hide nothing in my belongings to threaten national security.
I'm just trying to write a few lines.
Two or three words. Verses to make music in the ears of uninvited guests.
Words that if they have any power it won't be to free me.

Power to free.

And so from the shadows come these eyes like evoking a ghost. Names I'll forget.
Even if I refuse. Soon they'll come to be erased from my memory by the day's sour wine.
Urgently.
When I rub my head hard against the walls.
When I write verses to the changing seasons.
Far from the tropics. Things friends have told to stay out. Behind the bars of the soul where paper roses climb.

Iron flowers on the chest of a man.

Behind the bars. I attempt the start of "a return to my prison."
House where bats perch and suck blood on iron flowers.
A return to prison. Margarita's forbidden desires. The beautiful son vigorously bursting his sorrows on the pillow.
Death games. Children disputing the fruit of solitude like animals.
Outside, far from Ranel's eyes, beneath the lead weight of his expired moons, the Triptychs brown in some chapel of this world where God's forgotten him. And Juan too, who wanted to exist in distancing lovers.
Prisoner in oil paintings. With blue death. Shared. Writing to escape the body.
Armandito, rising like ice in a country of sun. Here nobody cries.
We're made of terracotta in the Spartan mother's prayers.
Through her veins a return to the island. Here everybody loves. And waits:
Here grow *the iron flowers: resounding like the chest of a man*.

Efecto café bulevar

Y todo está dispuesto de este modo,
para que no salgamos del mágico círculo.
Ossip Mandelstam

Para Ghabriel, una isla propia

Entro. Pido el último café. Elena Burke es un recuerdo.
Todo es frío bajo los toldos.
Por momentos la lluvia de tránsito nos obliga a adentrarnos.
Descendemos a otros arcos protectores.
Patio interior de piedra. Asfixiante.
Aquí se vive arduamente. Se hace un espacio
a cada provincia. Y otra se acerca mientras pides un café.
A cambio de una moneda tendrás la joya blanca
entre tus manos. Es amargo el trago para beberlo despacio.
Ha de ser despacio para que el trago baje amargo.
Y comienzas a conversar. Pues aquí se habla vivamente.
Interrumpidos por la mano que pide con hedor e insistencia.
(También mi mano es pobre y la guardo bajo la madera).

A veces soy interrogado como cualquier ciudadano
que bebe su café. Su trago amargo. Y respondo.
Me identifico con habilidad para no agotar el tiempo.
Bajo la luz todo es minuto tras minuto
un detenimiento innecesario. Una espiral que se verticaliza.
Y asciende. Asciende el humo del café.
Y justificas los desplomes. Demasiado recientes que somos.
De ayer mismo. Amar es una isla.
Y morir es adentrarse a la mar coagulada.
Un aroma de azucenas. Un estarse quieto bajo los toldos.
"De transparencia en transparencia" obnubilados.
Viejo Eliseo que bebes tu café. Tu trago amargo.

Café Bulevar Effect

*And it's all arranged, we never
break the magic circle*
Osip Mandelstam

For Ghabriel, an island unto himself

I go in. Order the last coffee. Elena Burke is a memory.
Everything's cold beneath the awnings.
Occasionally the rain in transit forces us in.
We descend toward other protective arches.
Inner stone courtyard. Stifling.
Living is hard work here. A space is made
for every province. And another comes closer while you order a coffee.
For small change you'll have the white jewel
in your hands. The drink's bitter for swallowing it slow.
It has to be slow so the drink goes down bitter.
And you start to chat. Since talking is intense here.
Interrupted by the begging hand rank and insistent.
(My hand's poor too. I keep it beneath the wood).

Sometimes I'm interrogated like any other citizen
having his coffee. His bitter pill. And I answer.
I skillfully identify myself so as not to use up the time.
Under the light everything's an unnecessary thoroughness
minute after minute. A spiral going vertical.
And up. The coffee steam floating up.
And you justify the collapses. Too recent as we are.
Only yesterday. To love is an island.
And to die is to go deep into the clotted sea.
A scent of lilies. A settle down beneath the awnings.
"From one transparence to another transparence" clouded.
Old Eliseo drinking your coffee. Your bitter pill.

Aquí vienen a morir los poetas.
Y un ángel fatigado vuela bajo otro cielo. Y otro ángel
comienza su discurso en el sopor de las fabulaciones.
Otro revienta su cabeza contra el asfalto.
Llora otro de rodillas. Y el "pez angelecido" se muere de tristeza.
Alza su vuelo bajo el cielo empedrado
de Madrid. Sin voz. Sin alas. "Hasta de espaldas se ve que está llorando".
Pero todavía hay tiempo.
Bebamos el último café mientras María Teresa nos canta.
Qué cante el Benny su página ruinosa.
Qué Bola sea una flor negra sobre el piano.
Qué Celeste rompa el adoquín con su paso.
Que aquí cada poeta tiene su caballo blanco.
Su leopardo. Su canario. Sus dos patrias.
Que el cuerpo de una isla no se sostiene sin un buen verso.
Pues sobrevivir bajo los toldos es una fiesta.
Y cada fragmento de imán transmuta en oro.
La Bella Cubana bebe en su Capilla de Cobre el trago de café.
Su trago amargo. (Transformada la medialuna
bajo sus mínimos pies el aroma de las mariposas
se confunde perversamente con el vuelo del colibrí).
Flota una tabla en la bahía. Es tiempo de pedir
por nuestras vidas. Y pedimos confusamente.
Casi sin darnos cuenta a cada paso.
"Flor de isla, tú te ofreces aromática y gentil
como una taza de café". Tú despides a la mujer coronada
con laureles –"ni libre es ni la prisión la encierra"–.
Sus huesos se pudren donde la tierra es menos blanca.

Porque en verdad nunca fueron tan importantes los poetas
como en este Café bajo los toldos. Decadentes. Y felices.
Pero de improviso algo se transforma tras las rejas.
Y te hace pensar que de nada sirvió la culpa
de Juan Clemente Zenea. El destierro de Heredia.
La muerte de Plácido. Las cartas de amor de Juana Borrero.
Ni el pulmón asfixiado de Lezama.
De nada sirvió que Julián del Casal se muriera de risa.
De nada ha servido escribir un buen poema

The poets come here to die.
And a weary angel flies beneath another sky. And another angel
begins his speech in the sleepiness of fabulations.
Another slams his head against the asphalt.
Another cries on his knees. And the "angelized fish" dies of sadness.
Takes his flight beneath the stony Madrid
sky. Voiceless. Wingless. "Even from the back you can tell he's crying".
But there's still time.
Let's have the last coffee while María Teresa sings.
Let Benny sing his ruinous page.
Let Bola be a black flower atop the piano.
Let Celeste crack the cobblestone with her step.
For here each poet has their white horse.
Their leopard. Their canary. Their two homelands.
For the body of an island won't hold without a good verse.
Since surviving beneath the awnings is a celebration.
And each magnet scrap turns to gold.
In her Copper Chapel the Bella Cubana drinks her coffee.
Her bitter pill. (The half-moon transformed
beneath her tiny feet the scent of butterflies
mixes perversely with the flight of the hummingbird).
A board floats in the bay. It's time to ask
for our lives. And we confusedly ask.
Almost not realizing with each step.
"Island flower, you offer yourself up fragrant and gracious
like a cup of coffee." You bid farewell to the woman crowned
in laurels –"not free not locked away"–.
Her bones rot where the earth is not as white.

Because honestly the poets were never as important
as in the Café beneath the awnings. Decadent. And happy.
Yet something suddenly transforms behind the bars.
And it makes you think that Juan Clemente Zenea's
guilt was meaningless. Heredia's exile.
Plácido's death. Juana Borrero's love letters.
Not even Lezama's stifled lung.
Meaningless that Julián del Casal died laughing.
Meaningless to have written a good poem

cuando Fina anuncia su "dulce nevada". Y la nieve
comienza a caer sobre los toldos.

Este Café no es el sitio de siempre.
El sol sobre el mármol blanco se evapora.
Y quiero marcharme. Escapar del frío. Esta no es mi sangre.
Prometo no regresar. (Vuelve el agua inmarcable
a la arena. El mar entre las tazas conforma
un plano alucinante). Sobre la mesa roja ya estoy de vuelta.
Ya entro a los círculos de hierro como un animal viciado.
Nuevamente. Y pido el último café. Y otro. Y otro…

when Fina proclaims her "sweet snowfall". And the snow
begins to fall upon the awnings.

This Café isn't the same old place.
The sun on the white marble vanishes.
And I want to leave. Escape the cold. This isn't my blood.
I promise not to return. (The unbiddable water returns
to the sand. The sea among the cups shapes
a beguiling plane). On the red table I've come back.
Now I go into the iron circles like an animal hooked.
Once more. I order the last coffee. And another. And another…

ISAILY PÉREZ GONZÁLEZ

Isaily Pérez González (Santa Clara, 1975) has published four books of poetry. Her work has appeared in influential anthologies of young Cuban poetry and has received numerous prizes, including Honorable Mention for the La Gaceta de Cuba Poetry Prize in 2014.

Centro Comercial de la 54

Del familiar cardumen se desprenden los niños
se sueltan a girar como derviches
se lanzan a las cercas: mira mami no hay cola
y los padres
(más bien quise decir los hombres)
las manos al bolsillo sacan algo:
un menudo un tiquete que los lance hasta el cielo
y cuando van cayendo a veces gritan
de miedo saludando: adiós míranos mami
cubiertos del helado bajarán de artefactos
que imitan la experiencia que no tendremos nunca:
un avión un caballo una casa de espejos.
Las pesadas bocinas se comieron las lenguas de organillo
y ahora lanzan su arenga: venga compre regrese
luego cantan un rato.
En mitad de las ferias
ocasiones habrá que te encuentre una mano
pues en la multitud difícil no rozar
no equivocarse.
Sin volverte a mirar tú querrás apretarla
pues qué mano ha de ser
sino la de tu madre que te estrecha en el tiempo
pero es solo otro niño confundido.
Entonces ves al perro
entre la multitud que traga las rositas
y hace fila por horas
comprando unos segundos de ese *algo*
de pronto has visto al perro sin correa
mirando temeroso los espacios que abre y cierra el cardumen
que pueden engullirlo como a sobras
y tienes que aguantarte respirar como puedas
pues nadie ha de saber
que en mitad de la noche de girantes corceles
de tacitas pintadas
la tierra se ha salido de su eje.

Mall on 54th Street

The children disentangled from the family shoal
let loose to whirl like dervishes
throw themselves to the fences: look mom no lines
and the fathers
(actually I mean the men)
hands in pockets pull something out:
a coin, a ticket to launch them to the heavens
and when they fall they sometimes scream
from fear, waving: bye-bye look at us mom
covered in ice cream they'll get off the artifacts
that simulate the experience we'll never have:
a plane, a horse, a house of mirrors.
The obnoxious loud speakers ate the hurdy-gurdy's tongues
and now let out their harangue: come on out buy something
come back soon
then they sing a while.
In the middle of the fair
on occasion a hand might find you
in the crowd it's hard not to touch
not be mistaken.
Without turning to see you'll want to grab hold
whose hand could it be
but your mother's reaching out over time
it's just another kid confused.
Then you see the dog
in the crowd gulping down popcorn
in line for hours
buying a few seconds of that *something*
suddenly you've seen the dog no leash
fearfully watching the spaces opened closed by the shoal
that might gobble him up like leftovers
and you have to hold yourself back, breathe anyway you can
no one needs to know
that in the middle of night spinning steeds
and tiny painted cups
the earth's come unhinged.

Prosperando en las ruinas

Amor inenarrable prosperando en las ruinas
la casa que era antaño de los chinos
ha visto pasar todo: *hermosura y espanto*
el deseo es mercurio tú sabes muy bien eso
el cielo de tu casa se ha izado noche a noche en lentejuelas.
Que los trozos de vidrio lo reproduzcan todo
como solo ellos saben
los pedazos de todo lastiman como vidrio
me miran con fijeza con sus ojos de pavos.
Nadie me dijo nunca que pasaría esto
el dolor me ha doblado con brutal elegancia
el mundo es un pañuelo que ha plegado sus puntas
conmigo allí en el centro
si me tomo su vino quizás logre dormirme.
Amor inenarrable
encuentra una razón que te resguarde
al regresar a casa –lo que entiendas por eso–
que no lastime tanto salir hacia el balcón
cuando ya es madrugada: tu momento en el mundo.
Vuelve al loto y al muérdago
en algún sitio hay uno donde bajo sus ramas
todo el amor jurado se besa para siempre.
He dicho las palabras que estaban prohibidas
quien pesa el corazón lo ha hallado insuficiente
y ya ascienden las aguas
retoños de mandrágora en los muros del relojero
alzan una pared que obliga a caminar más rápido.
Ya mi casa me parece inalcanzable:
cinco seis
siete cuadras en el tiempo.

Flourishing in Ruins

Indescribable love flourishing in ruins
the house that in years gone by belonged to the Chinese
has seen it all: *beauty and fear*
desire is mercury you know that very well
the sky in your house has risen up night after night in sequins.
Let the shards of glass recreate everything
like only they know how
the pieces of everything wound like glass
stare at me with their turkey eyes.
No one ever told me this would happen
the pain doubles me over with brutal elegance
the world is a handkerchief with its corners folded
with me there in the middle
if I drink some of its wine perhaps I can sleep.
Indescribable love
find a reason to shield you
when you get home –whatever that is for you–
so it doesn't hurt so much to go out on the balcony
when it's daybreak: your moment in the world.
Return to the lotus and the mistletoe
somewhere there's one where all sworn
love kisses beneath its branches for always.
I've said the forbidden words
whoever weighs the heart finds it's not enough
and now the waters rise
mandrake shoots in the watchmaker's walls
raise a barrier forcing us to walk faster.
Now my house seems unreachable:
five six
seven blocks in time.

La vida en otra parte

Mientras ando y llovizna
pienso la vida que no viviré en este sitio
ni en otro,
la vida que guardada he perdido
atesorada en balde como ciertas monedas en desuso.
Siempre
en algunas calles de La Habana y Santa Clara
pienso lo mismo:
un cuento de Borges
que trata de un jardín y sus bifurcaciones
y creo para mí
mientras ando la calle donde evito comer
decir mi nombre
para que nada quede ni se vaya conmigo.
Detrás de cualquier puerta
otra yo está haciendo cosas
que no puedo aceptar tranquilamente.

Life Elsewhere

As I walk under drizzle
I think about the life I won't live in this place
or in any other,
the life hung onto I've lost
kept around in vain like a few coins no longer in use.
Along certain streets in Havana and Santa Clara
I always
come back to the same:
a Borges story
about a garden and its forking
that I think are mine
as I walk the street where I won't eat
or say my name
so nothing will stay or go with me.
Behind a stray door
another I is doing things
I just can't put up with.

Bajo el poderío del miriñaque

La banda sonora ahoga toda respiración.
Te has dormido en mitad de la trama
cuando atentos los ojos persiguen en la pantalla
al flotante miriñaque.
Alguien enciende un cigarro y lo pasa al de su lado
luego otro.
El humo ayudaría al animal a esconder su predominio
tras las finas columnillas grisáceas.
Minúscula es tu mano medida contra mi mano
dormida aún retienes tu poder como una reina muerta.
El imperio del miriñaque
trasciende el cuadrado de vidrio
debajo de la franela acaricio mis músculos
todo posible sonido
es disonancia al compás de tu respiración
que acaso nadie escucha excepto yo.
Si no me vigilo estiraré una mano a esa silente densidad
al expuesto nacimiento de tu espalda
que admiro de soslayo.
Deberás abrir los ojos
para que junto al filoso acantilado
el animal se duerma y yo exhale libremente.
Me vuelvo a la trama
pero el deseo antepone figuras más extrañas
que el humo.
El deseo es un collar incandescente
que oprime mi garganta.
Toda la noche podría mirarte
y al amanecer indescriptible seguirías.
Así mismo te vi entrando
en la antigua fonda de los chinos
los faroles de pergamino se encendieron de súbito
con una luz distinta
y oí gritos que ordenaban sopas y otros platos
pero ya la violenta actualidad

Under the Power of the Crinoline

The soundtrack drowns out all the breathing.
You've fallen asleep in the middle of the plot
when attentive eyes follow the floating crinoline
on the screen.
Someone lights a cigarette and passes it to the one next to him
then another.
The smoke could help the animal to hide its predominance
behind the fine grayish columns.
Your hand is tiny up against my hand
even sleeping you hold your power like a dead queen.
The crinoline's empire
transcends the glass square
beneath the flannel I rub my muscles
every possible sound
is dissonance to the rhythm of your breathing
perhaps no one hears but me.
If I don't watch myself I'll stretch out a hand toward that silent density
the bare beginning of your back
I admire sideways.
You ought to open your eyes
so the animal might sleep and I can exhale freely
alongside the sharp cliff.
I return to the plot
but desire prefers stranger shapes
than smoke.
Desire is a luminous necklace
crushing my throat.
I could watch you all night
and in the morning you'd still be beyond words.
That's exactly how I saw you going into
the old Chinese dive
paper lanterns suddenly shining
with a different light
and I heard cries of orders for soups and other dishes
still the violent present

explotaba como un fuego de artificio sobre nosotros.
Vi tu salida y era imposible la idea de perderte
en la ordinaria multitud de Chinatown.
Toda la noche te estuve mirando
sin la esperanza de esta noche.
Al otro día las cosas hermosas me asumieron
florecía lo adventicio como si fuese la ciudad su estación
y el barrio de los chinos
giraba sus esquinas para encontrarnos.
Asomarse a la baranda
era verte pasar con los crípticos papeles bajo el brazo
yo buscaba la tramoya tras estos accidentes
y bajo la certeza de predestinación.
Las arañas de tu sala se encendieron
bajaste los peldaños de dos en dos hasta la calle
y ya era la segunda noche.
La trama se volvía imprevisible
mi sustancia estaba en vilo como ahora.
Sé que sabes el final
mientras cruzan por tu sueño flashazos de la ficción
aun en su mudez
temible es el poder de un miriñaque
que escapa de la pantalla
y cuelga sobre nosotros como una emplomada lámpara.
Despiertas cuando apagan sus cúpulas los cigarros
y sales a la noche de Chinatown.
Del torso del animal asciende la marea de los créditos.

went off like fireworks above us.
I saw you leave and the idea was impossible
losing you in the ordinary crowd of Chinatown.
All night I watched you
without tonight's hope.
The next day beautiful things took me over
the adventitious flowered as if the city were its season
and Chinatown
spun its corners to find us.
To lean over the railing
was to see you pass by with cryptic papers underarm
I looked for stage lifts behind these accidents
and beneath the sureness of fate.
The spiders in your living room caught fire
you went down the stairs two by two to the street
and it was the second night.
The plot turned unpredictable
my substance on tenterhooks like now.
I know you know the ending
while in your sleep crisscross bright fiction flashes,
still in its dumbness
the power of the crinoline is frightening
escaping the screen
hanging before us like a leaden lamp.
You wake up when cigarettes put out their domes
and leave for the Chinatown night.
From the animal's torso soars the tide of credits.

JAVIER MARIMÓN MIYARES

Javier Marimón Miyares (Matanzas, 1975) is a poet and playwright. He has published four books of poetry. A collection of short prose pieces and a play appeared in 2017. His work has been translated into English, German, and Italian. He currently lives in Puerto Rico.

Escritura de letra alfa (fragmentos)

4

Separante doctor de siamesas
Solo gracias recibe de una
Eso y nunca compartieron garganta
Y ambas querían andar separadas
¿Tendrá la boca de jugo llena?
Cuchillas entre ideas y motivos disecan.

11

Candidatos de supermercado sonríen nerviosos
A público posible. Con qué soltura, sin embargo
Conversan cajeros contratados de antes
Con clientes espontáneos, suspiran candidatos
Destruyen momento que dura poco y ya no brilla.

15

Algo da vueltas al 8, de 7 o atrás
Borroso como día que aprendiste
Los números; seguro llegas
Maestra manca te tocó
Es lo que da vueltas.

Letter Alpha Writing (excerpts)

4

Separating doctor of Siamese
Only thanks received from one
That and a throat never shared
And each wanted to be separated
Might the mouth with juice be full?
Knives among ideas and motives dissect.

11

Supermarket candidates nervously smile
To possible public. Still, how skillful
Cashiers hired from before converse with
Spontaneous customers, candidates breathe
Destroy moment not lasting long no longer shining.

15

Something goes round and round 8, from 7 or behind
Blurry like day you learned
The numbers; confident you arrive
One-handed teacher you ended up with
It's what goes round.

22

Frituras engañan: sin mucho adentro
De lo que tampoco te encantaba
¿Y si lo fuera?, placer sentido montones de veces
¿Por qué no dejarla caer simplemente?

32

Hacer, piel de vaca, monedero
¿Se activa ser de vaca al abrir zíper
A través de recuerdo del ano respirante
Cuando mordía yerba?
¿Retozará en ella sacando pedazos
De mierda de su monedero?

34

Baja pie de sofá, tienes cuidado
Con perrito invisible que ahí descansa
Mas al bajar pie ausente, destrozado
Por fiero perro de vecino
Ya no rozas perrito tendido.

38

¿A quién darle las gracias debería:
A uréter, que el orine demora
Tiempo que en calentarse tarda el agua
O a ente eléctrico del calentador
Rayo capturado, antes del baño?

22

Fritters are misleading: not much inside
Of what you didn't love anyway
And if it were? Pleasure felt tons of times
Why not let it simply fall?

32

To make, cowhide, coin purse
Is being made from cow activated when opening zipper
From memory of breathing anus
When it bit grass?
To frolic in the cow pulling out pieces
Of shit from its coin purse?

34

Lowers foot from sofa, you're careful
With little invisible dog resting there
But when lowering absent foot, destroyed
By fierce neighbor dog
You no longer graze dog stretched out.

38

To whom give thanks should I?
To ureter, the urine taking
Time it takes the water to warm up
Or to electric entity of heater
Lightning rod captured, before the bath?

40

Ilusiones de analfabetismo:
Alfabetizadores demoraban en río
Risas lejos de casa
Pensando en el papel pasé la tarde
Miré la noche sin una referencia
Vibraba toda circunstancia.

41

¿Es la nata fatiga de leche?
¿A qué vieja le gusta y agradece
Lo que no podemos divisar:
Empuja hacia afuera la curva
Que causa a la vieja el gustarle
Como, de nata, movimiento?

42

El de casco saluda el vacío gritando
Sin respuesta: no hay obra de construcción
Falta parte de la vía delante
De otra obra terminada consecuencia:
Lejana figura contesta.

43

Qué específico lugar donde arreglan mofles
Qué sabroso comen almuerzo, manos negras de mofle
Se miran, casi no creen: son tan específicos
Sus mecánicos cuerpos, ríen, irradian
Fantásticos oros de mofle.

40

Illiteracy illusions:
Literacy tutors lingered in river
Laughing far from home
Thinking about the paper I spent the evening
I watched the night without a reference
All circumstance quivering.

41

Is cream the weariness of milk?
What old woman likes and is thankful for
What we can't make out:
Pushes outward the curve
That causes the old woman's liking it
As, of cream, movement?

42

The one in the helmet greets the void shouting
Unanswered: there is no construction work
There's a part of the road missing up ahead
From another work finished consequence:
Distant figure answers.

43

What a specific place where they fix mufflers
How tastily they eat lunch, hands black from muffler
They look at each other, almost don't believe: they're so specific
Their mechanical bodies, laugh, give off
Fantastic muffler golds.

47

Por fuera, una hoja dejada volar
Cae en ojo trabajando materias
Lucha idea en ramos tajados
Abre luz en el ojo, por dentro.

48

Cae helado en pulóver de helado dibujado
Se derrite en tela que lo representa
"Mamá", llama el helado su esencia
Lengua en cuchara de lengua dibujada
Define fuerte núcleo de la tarde.

47

Outside, a leaf left to fly
Falls in eye working matters
Struggle idea in cut bouquets
Opens light in the eye, inside.

48

Ice cream falls on t-shirt with drawing of ice cream
Melts on fabric that represents it
"Mamá," calls the ice cream its essence
Tongue on spoon with drawing of tongue
Defines evening's powerful core.

Leyman Pérez García (Matanzas, 1976) is a poet and editor. He holds a degree in Library Sciences, Socio-Cultural Studies and Cuban Culture. He is managing editor of *Matanzas*, a journal of literature and the arts. He has published eleven books of poetry and his work has received numerous prizes. He lives in Matanzas.

En el secadero de almas

Gotea gotea gotea
gotea
gotea
gotea
el suero citostático
el rompe venas que va
que
    brán
        do
            te
lentamente
l e n t a m e n t e
mientras a tu lado
alguien comenta
del deterioro
del tiempo
de la crisis perpetua
en que se encuentra
la nación
y detrás
del nervioso cristal
llueve
pero el agua
no limpia
ni cura
la expresión
de vida
o muerte
en los rostros
y unos jóvenes
parecen felices
bajo la llovizna
sin pensar
cuánto dolor hay

a solo unos metros
de ellos
a solo unos metros

In the Drying Shed of Souls

Drips drips drips
drips
drips
drips
the cytostatic IV
the veinburster
cr
  ush
      ing
         you
slowly
s l o w l y
while next to you
someone talks
about decline
about time
about the endless crisis
the nation
finds itself in
and behind
the nervous pane
it's raining
still the water
doesn't cleanse
or cure
the expression
of life
or death
in faces
and some kids
seem happy
beneath the drizzle
not thinking
how much pain there is

just a few meters away
from them
just a few meters away

ya nadie llora
se han secado
los ojos
en el secadero
de almas
gotea
gotea
gotea
el suero citostático
hacia las extremidades
que abandonan
la horizontalidad
que corroe
a la carne
y al espíritu
gotea
hacia el espíritu
y el tronco
de la sombra
retoña
como un jagüey
madura sus raíces
en la roja intemperie
gotea
hacia el cuello
donde tu dolor
y el mío
están dibujados
gotea
gotea
gotea
y después no tienes
más angustia
no tienes más
sustancias
que recordar.

everyone's stopped crying
eyes
have dried
in the drying shed
of souls
drips
drips
drips
the cytostatic IV
toward the limbs
that desert
horizontality
eating away
at flesh
and spirit
drips
toward the spirit
and shadow's
trunk
sprouts once more
like a jagüey tree
ripens its roots
out in the red open
drips
toward the neck
where your pain
and mine
are drawn
drips
drips
drips
and later you have
no more anguish
you have no more
substances
to recall.

Los escogedores

leen en el arroz
lo mismo que la sangre lee en el cuerpo que nada puede escoger.
Cuentan los restos duros (coágulos, cielo desgarrado, astillas)
que entran a la boca con la misma intensidad
con que una raíz rompe el suelo huyendo de la naturaleza
que se deja pinchar con la sucia aguja de la nación.
Un cuerpo sin cabeza y sin extremidades. Un tronco enfermo.
Tierra abriendo la tierra donde crece Oscar Matzerath.
El humano con menos cenizas en Auschwitz y en el Morro-Cabaña.
Los escogedores de arroz a veces no leen nada. Entran y salen
como autistas que se buscan a sí mismos y se encuentran
en el hacha de talar la libertad, en la tierra abriendo la tierra
que hay en mí. Cerrándose, cerrándome.
Lo mismo que la sangre lee.

The Sorters

read in the rice
the same as what blood reads in the body that can't sort a thing.
They count the hard remains (clots, torn sky, splinters)
that pierce the mouth with the same intensity
as a root breaking through the soil fleeing the nature
that lets itself be pricked by the nation's dirty needle.
A body headless, limbless. A trunk diseased.
Earth opening the earth where Oskar Matzerath grows.
The human with the fewest ashes in Auschwitz and in the Morro-Cabaña.
The rice sorters sometimes don't read a thing. They come and go
like autistics in search of themselves and are found
in the axe to chop down freedom, in the earth opening the earth
in me. Closing themselves up, closing me up.
The same as what blood reads.

Antillas

Lo que aprendí es que existía un lugar llamado Antillas un lugar dentro de la geometría euclidiana donde el largo ancho y alto del cuerpo no tienen la misma serenidad Antillas crea una imagen de sí misma en cada uno de nosotros un objeto fractal contra otro "Ácida lluvia" dices mientras el propio signo lingüístico piensa en la función que debe ocupar Antillas del negro que conquista al blanco Antillas en el brocal donde todo comienza a ser un paisaje interminable como el de Gilles Deleuze que necesita del espacio para respirar el espacio o mejor el tiempo para respirar el tiempo que no está en Cuba ni en las menores y mayores contracorrientes que tragamos con dificultad Antillas imaginarias aguijoneándose sobre el olvidado Renacimiento sobre los viejos manuscritos de la imprenta aún con olor a continente Lo que aprendí es que existía un lugar llamado Antillas donde la tierra era pobre y exótica como la que algún día caerá sobre mí sin tocarme

West Indies

What I learned was that there was a place called the West Indies a place within Euclidian geometry where the length width and height of the body don't have the same serenity West Indies forms an image of itself in each of us a fractal object against another "Rain acid" you say while the linguistic sign itself thinks about the function it ought to take up West Indies of the black man who conquers the white man West Indies in the parapet where it all begins to be an unending landscape like Gilles Deleuze's needing space to breathe space or rather time to breathe time that is not in Cuba or in the lesser or greater countercurrents we struggle to swallow Imaginary West Indies spurring itself on over the forgotten Renaissance over the old manuscripts in the printing house still smelling of continent What I learned was that there was a place called the West Indies where the soil was poor and exotic just like the one that will fall over me someday without touching

La muerte de los objetos

Los objetos contienen la posibilidad
de todos los estados de cosas.

Ludwig Wittgenstein

En el boulevard de Obispo
pobres almas
hombres-hilos
que no entran
por el hueco de la aguja
costuras descosidas
remiendos
mentes descosidas
almas muertas
que se cosen la boca
para que no salga
oscuridad —diría Dostoievski
mientras se arrastra por el subsuelo
mordiéndose la lengua
caminando en círculos
mordiéndose las ausencias

en la primera está el tirano padre
hacha en la frente
hormiga en la boca
antes de llover y
después que la sequía llegó
a la casa
que no tiene por qué
parecerse al sol
materia que falta
como en un trapecio mudo
para el hombre sin piernas
que luchó en las guerras de otros

The Death of Objects

*Objects contain the possibilities
of all states of affairs.*

Ludwig Wittgenstein

On Obispo Boulevard
poor souls
men-threads
who don't go
through the eye of the needle
unstitched seams
patches
unstitched minds
dead souls
who've sewn their mouths
so darkness
doesn't come out –Dostoyevsky would say
while he drags himself along the subsoil
biting his tongue
walking in circles
biting his absences

in the first is the father tyrant
ax on his forehead
ant in his mouth
before raining and
after the drought got
to the house
that has no reason
to look like the sun
missing matter
like in a mute trapeze
for the legless man
who fought in someone else's wars

y ahora es un fragmento de metralla
olvidado
enterrado en sí mismo
almas muertas que piden
permiso para respirar
luz
falta luz en todo
en la última ausencia
era un invidente
y ponía los dedos
sobre el dolor
bajo la tierra
que da frutos podridos
robados con miedo
tragados con miedo
en el boulevard de Obispo
almas muertas
gusanos de seda
lana de ovejas
plantas de algodón
¿qué he dicho
       que no tenga ausencias?
objetos sin vida —diría Dostoievski

and is now a fragment of forgotten
shrapnel
buried in himself
dead souls ask
for permission to breath
light
no light anywhere
in the last absence
was a blind man
and he placed his fingers
on the pain
beneath the earth
bearing rotten fruit
stolen with fear
swallowed with fear
on Obispo Boulevard
dead souls
silk worms
sheep's wool
cotton plants
what have I said
          that doesn't have absences?
lifeless objects –Dostoyevsky would say

MARCELO MORALES CINTERO

Marcelo Morales Cintero (Havana, 1977) is a poet and prose writer. He received a degree in History from the University of Havana and graduated from the Univercitá per Stranieri di Perugia, Italia with a degree in Italian Language and Culture. He has published three books of poetry –all prize-winning– and a novella. A collection of his work, *The World as Presence*, recently appeared in English. He lives in Havana.

Materia (fragmentos)

Cuando veo el polvo en mi cuarto flotando, pienso en la sentencia, hundo mi cara en él.
✦

Nosotros, los humanos, hemos construido lo real,
lo hemos idealizado. En el bar, en la barra, mi percepción del tiempo, mi vida, la búsqueda del amor sin cese.
De eso se trata, me digo, de un fracaso tras otro,
de estar de nuevo en el vacío que produce.
En la calle, en el carro, el viento y las luces en la cara,
luces que pasan, vida que pasa, movimiento.
✦

Al mundo uno lo siente. Estás adentro, me digo, en un fragmento las cosas se definen, entrar en el círculo tiene ese significado, el polvo flota, luz. En la taza de café no veo la taza sino el hueco.
✦

Yo vivo con dolor. Atravieso las calles con dolor. El pasado dura lo que de él puedes recordar. El pasado son minutos.
✦

El mundo y la gente te imprimen su energía.
Energía en el recuerdo y en los sentimientos. Energía en las sensaciones. El mundo se siente, contaminación, eso es lo humano, charcos en la calle, barrio chino. Tus ojos recorren lo real, se van de un segundo a otro, tu cuerpo, de un segundo a otro, tu mente, eso es estar vivo, un lugar y luego otro.
✦

Me levanto y veo, en el espejo, algunas manchas. Naturaleza del retorno. El amor en su punto último es el vacío, apréndete eso, me digo. Me levanto en el desierto, cambio las sábanas.
✦

Tengo miedo de la luz en el cristal, aire que entra en la ventana, polvo cubriendo los objetos, la sensación, la búsqueda de la sensación sin cese. Una cuchara metálica en el borde de la mesa, una silla rota, hay una presencia aquí. Lo poético provee de una conciencia en medio de los días. Bajo las escaleras, subo las escaleras, mis ojos tienen la apertura. No hay significado pero hay símbolo, tiempo corriendo en lo real, conciencia.

Matter (excerpts)

When I see the dust in my room floating, I think of the maxim, sink my face into it.

※

We humans have built what's real,
we've idealized it. In the bar, at the bar, my perception of time,
my life, the ceaseless search for love.
That's what it's about, I tell myself, from one failure to the next,
once more in the void it produces.
On the street, in the car, wind and lights on my face,
passing lights, passing life, movement.

※

One feels the world. You're inside, I tell myself, in a fragment things are defined, to set foot in the circle has that meaning, dust floats, light. In the coffee cup I don't see the cup I see the hollow.

※

I live in pain. Cross the streets in pain. The past lasts as long as what you can remember of it. The past is minutes.

※

The world and the people stamp their energy on you.
Energy in memory and feelings. Energy in sensations. The world feels, contamination, that is what's human, puddles in the street, Chinatown. Your eyes look over what's real, flutter from one second to the next, your body, from one second to the next, your mind, that's being alive, one place and then another.

※

A void can act over another void. The universe is its production.

※

I get up and see some spots in the mirror. Nature of the return. Love at its ending point is the void, keep that in mind, I tell myself. I get up in the desert; I change the sheets.

※

I'm afraid of the light in the glass, air coming in through the window, dust covering objects, the sensation, the ceaseless search for sensation. A metallic spoon on the edge of the table, a broken chair, there's a presence here. What's poetic supplies a consciousness amid the days. I go downstairs, I go upstairs, my eyes have the opening. There's no meaning but there's a symbol, time running in what's real, consciousness.

❧

Yo no sé dónde se van los que se mueren, los que te amaron, yo no sé. La memoria de ti será eliminada. El susurro de su saya cuando cerraba la puerta.

❧

Subo los peldaños palpando la baranda, toco el metal del picaporte, hago la llave girar. No existe nada entre lo vivo y lo muerto. En el patio la luz cae medio roja, peldaños amarillos. La vida se comporta sin conciencia. Esto es el mundo, materia, materia, y nada más.

❧

Corren todos en la misma dirección, por más que se alejen, todos van allá de nuevo. Llueve. En el cristal, los discursos del agua se hacen complicados, una luz, todo gira en torno al cero, el centro del mundo en el que siempre has pensado.

❧

El río y no el mar, tiene destino. El mundo, un fragmento de mis ojos. Columnas sucias, tubos de escape, humo, el cielo, un cerebro corrompido. Materia gris.

❧

Lo poético tiende a lo sobrenatural, paso del tiempo. Dios como un tubo de luz fría. Caminas en la noche y piensas: el aire está cargado de bacterias, la vida está para ser superada. La araña teje un problema circular, *Al menos por un momento, el insecto será un guerrero seguro de su victoria.* Las cosas que están en el tiempo son cosas que están en el espacio.

❧

La materia solo existe en el presente, las personas. Me esperaba siempre en el café cuando caía la tarde. Yo salía de las clases, atravesaba las calles por verla. Nos separaba el espacio y no el miedo. El amor no está aquí para ser olvidado. A veces me acuerdo de ella, a veces me olvido.

❧

Cosas que entran y salen de la vida, otro lado del cual cruzar a este, una mariposa fea, quedó inmóvil. Eres testigo de las muertes ajenas. La clave de esta obra está en su concepción. Toda esta materia, que piensa y siente la materia.

❧

En la vida el dolor y el placer son instantáneos. Mi especie llegó al conocimiento atómico. La Habana -calor- agosto. Nuestro miedo más grande no es la muerte, la muerte es nuestra fantasía. Papeles sucios en las calles. Gente, mar que choca contra el muro, vivir para llegar a ese destino.

→←

I don't know where those who die go, those who loved you, I don't know. The memory of you will be erased. The soft sighing of her skirt when she'd close the door.

→←

I climb the steps, feeling the handrail, touch the metal of the door latch, make the key turn. Nothing exists between the living and the dead. On the patio light falls half red, yellow steps. Life behaves unconsciously. This is the world, matter, matter and nothing more.

→←

They all run in the same direction, the more they wander off, they all go there once more. It's raining. On the glass the water's discourses grow complicated, a light, everything spins around zero, the center of the world where you've always thought.

→←

The river, not the sea, has a destination. The world, a fragment of my eyes. Dirty columns, exhaust pipes, smoke, sky, a corroded brain. Gray matter.

→←

What's poetic tends toward the supernatural, time's passing. God like a florescent light bulb. You walk in the night and think: the air is heavy with bacteria, life is to be exceeded. The spider weaves a circular problem, *At least for a moment the insect will be a warrior assured of its victory.* Things in time are things in space.

→←

Matter only exists in the present, persons. She always waited for me in the café when evening fell. I'd get out of class, cross streets to see her. Space separated us, not fear. Love isn't here to be forgotten. Sometimes I remember her, sometimes I forget.

→←

Things coming and going in life, another side to cross toward this one, an ugly butterfly, lingered motionless. You are witness to other deaths. The key to this work is in its conception. All this matter that matter thinks and feels.

→←

In life, pain and pleasure are instantaneous. My species came to atomic knowledge. Havana –heat– August. Our greatest fear isn't death, death is our fantasy. Dirty papers on the streets. People, sea crashing against the wall, living to reach that destiny.

❖

Las masas desembocan en un río. No conozco la nada y la nada me preocupa. Temo lo que todos temen. Cuando un gran cuerpo se hunde. El remolino lo sigue como si fuese su objetivo.

❖

Hay cosas que crecen del dolor. El tiempo para ti es la vida. Cosas en el espacio, eso es el mundo.

❖

Al mundo no le es difícil destruirte, la bomba está dentro, un reloj que se programa. Conexiones invisibles. Estás expuesto, el humano está siempre expuesto. La novia más larga, la más fría, llega siempre, se anuncia, siempre.

❖

Densidad mental, cuando la tormenta en el cielo, algo negro con nubes, psicológico, nubes psicológicas, una materia mental, vapor. No tengo conciencia de mi vida, tengo conciencia de mi angustia. Sobre la sábana pasa la noche, el universo frío, las estrellas. Uno siempre se pregunta a dónde fue a parar lo que vivió. Uno siempre se pregunta. Pensar que lo bello se destruye, pensar que lo bello se destruye. Materia desechable. Hay una profunda relación entre lo que hemos hecho y lo que haremos. Para que se cumpla un destino, todo debe estar en un tiempo exacto en un lugar exacto. En el futuro mi pensamiento no tendrá cuerpo donde enterrarse. Cuando meo creo que son piedras preciosas lo que tengo. Hay una carne ahí, hay una carne.

❖

A veces las estatuas necesitan cubrirse de una pátina, colores que solo el tiempo enciende, respuestas que son cosas de futuro. Hay cosas que solo dios entiende, hay un lenguaje de dios, hay un lenguaje. La vida tiene, para cada uno, sus respuestas.

❖

También el miedo salva. Estaba buscando algo que nunca pude tocar. No volvemos más que en el espacio, en el tiempo uno nunca vuelve.

❖

El tiempo tiene su lenguaje, la nostalgia siempre es cosa del presente. Cuando miras al horizonte, estás más cerca de ti, estás más cerca.

❖

Un rayo que entraba por la ventana alumbró mi mano. En la palma, al centro, sentí el peso de la luz. Permanecer oscuro es muy fácil, me digo. Lo contrario es lo difícil.

❖

Cuando dejes de tenerle miedo a la oscuridad vas a estar iluminado.

꧁꧂
The masses flow into a river. I don't know nothingness and nothingness worries me. I'm scared of what everyone is scared of. When a great body sinks. The whirlpool follows it as if it were its goal.
꧁꧂
There are things that swell from pain. Time for you is life. Things in space, that is the world.
꧁꧂
It's not hard for the world to destroy you, the bomb's on the inside, a timer set. Invisible connections. You're exposed, humans are always exposed. The longest, the coldest bride always arrives, gives notice, always.
꧁꧂
Mental density, when the storm in the sky, something black with clouds, psychological, psychological clouds, a mental matter, steam. I'm not conscious of my life, I am conscious of my anguish. Night, cold universe, stars cross over the sheet. One always wonders where what was lived ended up. One always wonders. To think the beautiful is destroyed, to think the beautiful is destroyed. Disposable matter. There's a deep relationship between what we've done and what we'll do. So a destiny can be reached, everything ought to be at an exact time in an exact place. In the future my thought won't have a body to be buried in. When I piss I think it's precious stones I have. There's a flesh there, there's a flesh.
꧁꧂
Sometimes statues need to be covered with a patina, colors only ignited by time, answers that are things from the future. There are things only god understands, there's a language of god, there's a language. Life has, for each of us, its answers.
꧁꧂
Fear also saves. I was searching for something I could never touch. We don't go back again except in space, in time one never goes back.
꧁꧂
Time has its language, nostalgia is always something from the present. When you watch the horizon you're closer to you, you're closer.
꧁꧂
A ray coming in through the window lit up my hand. In my palm, in the middle, I felt the weight of light. To stay dark is very easy, I tell myself. The opposite is what's hard.
꧁꧂
When you stop being afraid of the dark you'll be enlightened.
꧁꧂

❖

Uno no es solo lo que es, uno también es lo que ama. En la calle observo el mundo. Cada una de las cosas tiene más sentido que cualquiera de mis pensamientos.

❖

Uno tiene la responsabilidad para con uno mismo y con el mundo, de embellecer.
El amor es cosa de gente fuerte, la gente débil, se defiende con cinismo.
Uno tiene la responsabilidad para con uno de iluminarse, para con el mundo.
Pongo flores en un vaso, colocar ahí la función, la categoría del objeto.

❖

Cuando veo el polvo en mi cuarto flotando, pienso en la sentencia, hundo mi cara en él.

→←
One isn't only what he is, one is also what he loves. On the street I observe the world. Each of the things makes more sense than any of my thoughts.
→←
One has the responsibility, to himself and the world, to beautify.
Love is for the strong, the weak defend themselves with cynicism.
One has the responsibility to himself to be enlightened, to the world.
I place the flowers in a vase, put the function there, the category of object.
→←
When I see the dust in my room floating, I think of the maxim, sink my face into it.

De *El mundo como objeto*

Cuando la planta murió la sacaron del jarrón
y el lugar quedó vacío.

Nosotros, como antes sus raíces,
atrapados en la oscuridad
sentimos la presión.

→←

Lanzo una piedra.
Su recorrido es lo que hay entre yo y la realidad.
Nada más.
Este muro que deseo.
Cerrar los ojos
quedarme quieto.

→←

A veces temo a esos momentos en que sé
podría voltearme y caminar sobre mis pasos.
Yo bailaría desnudo en aquel cuarto
y ella riendo ordenaría la cama.

La radio de la cabecera continúa en mí sonando,
hubiese podido ser de otra manera,
fabricarme otro destino.
Lo que amamos no decide cuando acaba,
no querré ya recordar.

A veces temo esos momentos,
yo bailaría desnudo en aquel cuarto,
y ella riendo
               ordenaría la cama.

→←

From *The World as Object*

When the plant died they pulled it out of the pot
and the space was left empty.

We, like its roots before,
trapped in darkness,
feel the pressure.

→←

I throw a stone.
Its journey is what there is between me and reality.
Nothing more.
This wall I desire.
To close my eyes
sit still.

→←

Sometimes I'm scared of those moments when I know
I could turn around and go back over my steps.
I'd dance naked in that room
and laughing she'd tidy the bed.

The radio on the headboard still plays in me,
I could've been a different way,
built another destiny.
What we love doesn't decide when it ends,
Soon I won't want to remember.

Sometimes I'm scared of those moments,
I'd dance naked in that room
and laughing
         she'd tidy the bed.

→←

A veces hay esos momentos en que
bajas de noche una escalera
y no sabes si es un sueño,
o caminas por una calle vacía
cuando la luz de un bombillo cae sobre una planta marchita.
O duermes
y en la noche oyes,
el sonido de un ventilador que gira solo,
una tos seca que se sale de tu cuerpo,
o piensas en la ventanilla trasera de un tren
mientras el aire llega en bloque hasta tu rostro.
Afuera la ciudad,
las cosas que parecen siempre ajenas.

A veces hay esos momentos
en que entiendes
que la vida es un detalle.
Una mancha en la pared.
O ese hueco del lavamanos por donde se escurre el agua
y que miras espantado.

→←

Tengo que desechar el lenguaje,
la búsqueda de una "poética".
Penetro en sentido para encontrar la fuente.
Las palomas vuelan, se posan en los aleros.
Ellas también son parte del sistema.
Para mí todo es posible.
Todo,
con excepción de la muerte.
Estar solo es propio de la escritura.
Se necesita mucho dolor para entenderlo.

Sometimes there are moments when
you go down a staircase at night
and you don't know if it's a dream
or you walk down an empty street
when the light from a bulb falls on a withering plant.
Or you're asleep
and in the night you hear
the sound of a fan oscillating by itself,
a dry cough emerging from your body,
or you think about the back window of a train
while the air rushes in toward your face.
Outside the city
things that always seem strange.

Sometimes there are those moments
when you understand
life is a detail.
A stain on the wall.
Or the hole in the sink where the water goes down
that you gaze at terrified.

→←

I have to get rid of language,
the search for a "poetics."
I pierce sense to find the source.
Doves fly, perch on eaves.
They too are part of the system.
For me everything's possible.
Everything,
except death.
Being alone is unique to writing.
You need so much sorrow to understand that.

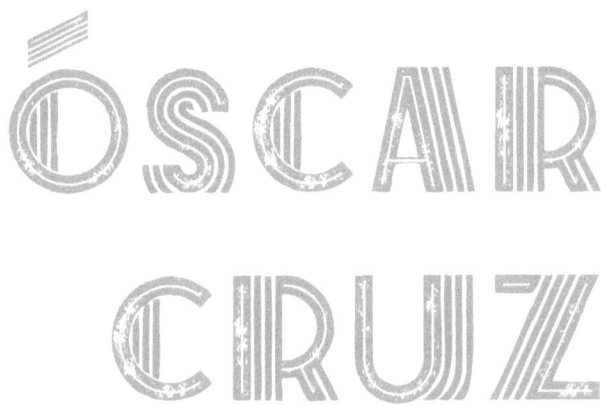

ÓSCAR CRUZ

Óscar Cruz (Santiago de Cuba, 1979) has published five books of poetry, the latest being *La Maestranza* (2014). He holds a degree in History from the Universidad de Oriente. He is the co-editor of the prestigious literary journal, *La noria*. He lives in Santiago de Cuba.

Los años de aprendizaje

cuando mi madre
me daba por la espalda
un cintarazo, yo solía
maldecirla en mis

adentros. "guárdate
esas lágrimas, pendejo,
para el día que te hagan
falta. esto es para que

aprendas a portarte
como un hombre". tenía
la violencia fácil. ganas
de enseñarme, como

recta Makarenko.
el lenguaje de los golpes
era hermoso. mi madre
a media voz, con un cinto

entre las manos, diciendo
grandes cosas. mi madre
(azotes que penetran
con más precisión que

un taladro en la madera.)
mi madre —planos fijos—,
imágenes cortas y largas,
cuerpo parado frente a mí

diciendo: "respétame,
carajo". veamos: escucho,
pero nunca entiendo. me
sobrevienen unas ganas

The Years of Learning

when my mother
would beat my back
with her belt, i'd often
curse her on the

inside. "hold back
those tears, asshole,
for when you'll need
them. this is so

you'll learn to act
like a man." she had
an easy violence. eager
to teach me, like

strict Makarenko.
the language of the blows
was beautiful. my mother
in a whisper, with a belt

in her hand, saying
great things, my mother
(lashes penetrating
more precisely than

a drill into wood.)
my mother —static shots—,
close up and long images,
body standing in front of me

saying, "respect me
damn it." let's see: i listen
but never understand. what
suddenly comes to me are great

enormes de matar que me
ponen siempre en entredicho.
mi madre, con el cinto
entre las manos,

tuvo la razón. el montón
de estiércol soy yo. la voz
del excremento soy yo. el
rostro del que orina soy yo.

soy el santo y el gachón.
madre, quiero que me cantes
la canción aquella del payaso.
sin perder la paciencia
ni el orgullo, cántame.
si no te la sabes, búscate una.
sé que no servías para el canto,
sin embargo, el cinto,

lo recuerdas. otros
para mí cantaron. guardo
nítidos detalles. para el uso,
restos del amor. tenías

el pelo cano, y el talle
esbelto. casi yo te amaba.
pero [...], ahora estoy
tranquilo. como un buey

que duerme bajo la lluvia,
duermo y sueño al lado de
mi madre. su presencia, sin
embargo, no es presencia

del mal. no conozco infancia
más amena... que aquella que
erigí bajo los golpes. digo
esto alegremente: palabras

desires to kill always
calling me into question.
my mother, with the belt
in her hand,

was right. the pile
of manure i am. the voice
of excrement i am. the
face of a man urinating i am.

i am saintly and spoiled.
mother, i want you to sing me
that song about the clown.
no losing patience
or pride, sing to me.
if you don't know it, find another.
i know you weren't good at singing
but the belt

you remember. others
sang for me. i recall
details so clearly. for my use,
remains of love. you had

gray hair and a slender
waist. i almost loved you.
but [...], now i'm
still. like an ox

asleep beneath the rain,
i sleep and dream alongside
my mother. her presence
though, isn't the presence

of evil. i don't know a more pleasant
childhood... than the one
i built beneath the blows. I say
this happily: words

que no ahogan,
que no admiten otro reino
de palabras. prosiguen sin
dolor, de manera que el dolor

se torna deseable. este
que soy, cobarde aceptación
de lo que fui, como un buey que
duerme bajo la lluvia,

contempla una pequeña flor
crecida en el estanque. tú
lo sabes, perdida flor, perdida
madre. como a un niño

que no entiende otro
lenguaje. a todo el que
me da su amor, le suelo
propinar su cintarazo.

that don't drown,
that don't accept another realm
of words. they persist
painlessly and so pain

becomes desirable. the one
i am, cowardly acceptance
of what i was, like an ox
asleep beneath the rain,

contemplates a small flower
growing in the pond. you
know, lost flower, lost
mother. like a boy

who doesn't understand another
language. everything
that loves me i tend
to beat with her belt.

Lo que cuenta

lo que cuenta es estar parado ahí,
en el borde de las gradas.
los perros frente a ti ladrando.
perros entrenados en el arte de matar.
perros welters con más de treinta libras.
(me gustaba estar ahí). la gente que viene
a estos lugares resulta interesante.
gente desahuciada con un rostro sin vida.
gente que viene por amor: amor a los zapatos,
amor a la ropa, amor al desastre;
y el desastre con su fuerza comenzaba
a interesarme.

los perros en su esencia eran bellos.
más bellos que mis padres,
más bellos que Dios. tenían rojas lenguas
y una forma masculina de babear.
sentí que mi vida estaba ligada a aquella baba,
a aquella forma envilecida de mirarse.
entonces saqué doscientos pesos
y se los puse al perro-nadie, un perro que nunca
había peleado y que lo haría contra uno
que sumaba dieciséis.
un perro invicto y secular como un gobierno.
comenzaron a matarse,
las bocas producían hechos de sangre.
instantes de duro placer.
perros que peleaban por lo posible
y lo imposible del hombre.
miraba las gradas y veía rostros brutales
de gente enajenada, feliz.
gente apostando a un cachorro sin vida.
al cabo de varios minutos
el perro al que había apostado ganó.
subido encima del otro ladraba una y otra vez.

What Counts

what counts is being there,
on the edge of the stands.
the dogs barking in front of you.
dogs trained in the art of killing.
welterweight dogs more than thirty pounds.
(i liked being there). the folks who come
to these places are interesting.
folks terminally ill with lifeless faces.
folks who come out of love: love of shoes
love of clothes, love of disaster;
and disaster with its force began
to appeal to me.

the dogs were in their essence beautiful.
more beautiful than my parents,
more beautiful than God. they had red tongues
and a masculine way of drooling.
i felt like my life was bound to that drool,
to that depraved way of looking.
so i pulled out two hundred pesos
and put them on the nobody dog, a dog that had never
fought against another
who'd been in sixteen.
a dog unbeaten and secular like a government.
they began to kill each other,
their mouths making violent crime.
instants of hard pleasure.
dogs fighting for what's possible
and impossible for man.
i looked at the stands and saw brutal faces
of deranged, happy folks.
folks betting on a lifeless pup.
after a few minutes
the dog i'd bet on won.
on top of the other it wouldn't stop barking.

lo cargaron como a un héroe y volvimos
en turba hacia la casa. íbamos callados.
escuchando cómo ríen, cómo hablan
los que ganan.
esa tarde supe lo que era un perdedor.
vi al perro derrotado en una jaba
sobre el borde del camino.
qué importa que hubiera ganado dieciséis.
la gloria en estos sitios dura poco.
y eso es lo que cuenta.
poco amor o poca vida no es tan malo.
lo que cuenta es saber que has apostado.
que has venido como ellos hasta aquí,
que has venido en la turba a darle diente
a la carne envejecida del amor.

it was carried off like a hero and the mob
headed back home. we were silent.
listening to how the winners
laugh, how they speak.
that evening i knew what a loser was.
i saw the defeated dog in a plastic bag
on the side of the road.
it didn't matter that he'd been in sixteen.
the glory in these places doesn't last long.
and that's what counts.
not much love or not much life isn't so bad.
what counts is knowing you've bet.
that you've come here like them,
that you've come here with the mob to sink your teeth
into the aged flesh of love.

El Mal y la Montaña
(Apuntes para una Teoría de la Invasión)

la Montaña
y todo lo que ella
representa.

la Montaña
tal y como fue: sin vacas
sin Reginos ni rebeldes.

la Montaña
que yo sigo y que me sigue
y que extiendo tras de mí
al caminar.

miro en dirección del Basurero
y sé que por allí se extiende
la Montaña.

es un privilegio haber nacido
y vivir en un lugar tan cercano
a la Montaña.

nada como un sitio
que cada día asciende un escalón
en el camino de su propia decadencia;
una región cada vez más provinciana,
gobernada por equipos sucesivos
de incapaces.

hace varios años subí a la Montaña.
vagando en sus praderas
conocí a tres o cuatro montañeses
que de tanto creer en la Montaña
perdieron el juicio y la vergüenza.

no hacían otra cosa que cagarse.
otros venían y enlataban y hacían

Evil and Mountain
(Notes on a Theory of Invasion)

Mountain
and all it
represents.

Mountain
just as it was: no cows
no Reginos or rebels.

Mountain
i follow and that follows me
and that i spread out behind me
as i walk.

i look in the direction of Garbage Dump
and i know that there spreads out
Mountain.

it's a privilege to have been born
and live in a place so close
to Mountain.

nothing like a place
that each day takes one more step
on the path of its own decadence,
a region more and more provincial,
governed by successive teams
of incompetents.

years ago I climbed Mountain.
wandering through its prairies
i met two or three highlanders
who after so much believing in Mountain
lost their wits and their shame.

they did nothing but shit themselves.
others came and canned it and turned

plusvalía aquella mierda.
hombres decididos a morir o prosperar.
juntos escribimos un poema
que describe el modus operandi
de ciertos cagadores encargados
del verdor en la Montaña.

el poema llegó hasta el despacho
de Magníficos Decentes
que pronto la tomaron con sus tropas.
el hecho trascendió como "La Toma
de la Montaña por los Decentes",
un hecho que hace las delicias
de los críticos de hoy.
no se sabe qué pasó
con aquellos cagadores. lo cierto
es que cambió la concepción,
de pronto se veían en las calles
gordas vacas y tres o cuatro neorrebeldes
con los cuales compartí
aquel poema.

ahora sí da gusto ascender a la Montaña,
contemplarla como es, aunque sepas
que no es más
que una extensa mentira verde,
demolida y puesta a funcionar en el poema
una y otra vez.

pero
como el tiempo ha consagrado a la Montaña,
como el pueblo no podría
vivir sin la Montaña,
sería peligroso suprimirla de una vez.
dejemos de momento intacta a la Montaña,
solo con pequeñas correcciones.

no sea que por culpa de un poema
los Decentes nos ataquen
otra vez.

that shit into surplus value.
men determined to die or prosper.
together we wrote a poem
describing the modus operandi
of certain shit-takers in charge
of the greenness of Mountain.

the poem made it to the office
of the Magnificently Decent
who took Mountain over with their troops.
the incident became known as "The Taking
of Mountain by the Decent,"
an incident that delights
today's critics.
no one knows what happened
to those shit-takers. yet the truth
is that it changed the conception,
suddenly on the streets you'd see
fat cows and three or four neo-rebels
with whom i shared
that poem.

now it really is quite pleasant to go up Mountain,
contemplate it as it is, even though you know
it's nothing more
than a huge green lie,
demolished and put to work in the poem
over and over.

yet
since time has enshrined Mountain,
since the people couldn't
live without Mountain,
it would be dangerous to abolish it once and for all.
for the moment let's leave Mountain intact,
just with some small modifications.

god forbid a poem be the reason
the Decent attack us
one more time.

LIUVAN HERRERA CARPIO

Liuvan Herrera Carpio (Fomento, 1981) is a poet, literary scholar and critic, and editor. He received a degree in Literature from the Central University in Las Villas and in Latin American Culture from the University for the Arts. He is currently a professor at the National University of Chimboraz. He has published four books of poetry and two books of essays. He lives in Riobamba, Ecuador.

Codorniz

Un aguacero de codornices decapitadas lapida el hambre a los que cruzan el desierto. Una lluvia de pájaros sin cabeza es una lluvia sin cabeza. ¿Qué bosque quedó sin trino, qué bosque sin primavera?
Mientras el peregrino despluma las gotas, la arena se contenta como un perro al recibir los pétalos del ave que lentamente se deshojan.
El peregrino es el marinero del desierto. Tras la tormenta de codornices naufragó: no ha podido soportar tanta arena en pleno vuelo.

Quail

A downpour of decapitated quail stone the hunger of those crossing the desert. A rain of headless birds is a headless rain. What forest was left with no song, what forest with no spring?
While the pilgrim defeathers the drops, the sand is as happy as a dog taking in the bird petals slowly plucked.
The pilgrim is the desert sailor. After the quail storm he shipwrecked: he hasn't been able to stand so much sand midflight.

Tigre

para Virgilio, antes de ser devorado

La piel del tigre es una trampa. Cuando mi hijo abre los ojos, como un grito frente al animal, no se da cuenta que tras un doble enrejado la piel del tigre está sin pintar. Los tigres desayunan carne de poeta: el domador castiga a las legumbres ofreciéndolas como armadura para este exquisito brazo de Blake que ahora mismo vemos engullir.

La digestión del tigre es paciente como los ojos de mi hijo, como los huérfanos ojos de mi hijo.

Tiger

for Virgilio, before being devoured

The tiger skin is a trap. When my son opens his eyes, like a shriek before the animal, he doesn't realize that behind the double trellis the tiger skin isn't painted. Tigers eat poet flesh for breakfast: the tamer punishes the legumes offering them up like a garnish for this exquisite Blake arm we now see being wolfed down.
The tiger's digestion is patient like my son's eyes, like my son's orphan eyes.

Camello

para Teresa, ahogada en el mar del camello

Este bisoño ejemplar ha nacido en la hora de su madre traspasar la aguja. Situación lacerante pues el embarazo no está relacionado en los anaqueles para la prueba. Nacer durante el ojo de la aguja ha dado al animal un peculiar carisma: cuando algún jinete lo castiga tras morder el espejismo de la hierba, acto seguido en la garganta del jinete se atraviesa una aguja que no precisamente es un espejismo. El agua viaja montañosa en la espalda del camello, éste, nos lanza ahora una carcajada de sal: es feliz y lo sabe: es el único animal que lleva un mar adentro.

Camel

for Teresa, drowned in the camel sea

This exemplary beginner was born when its mother went through the needle. A painful experience since pregnancy isn't mentioned on the trial shelves. To be born in the eye of the needle has given the animal a certain charisma: when a rider punishes him for biting the grass mirage, straightaway in the rider's throat pierces a needle that isn't exactly a mirage. Water travels mountain-like on the camel's back, this one lets out a salty guffaw: he's happy and he knows it: he's the only animal who carries a sea within.

Mortaja de sábado

Al tender las sábanas
como cuerpos recién ahogados,
una camisa contigua
encoge los hombros.
La ungida, sin nombre digno que recordar;
ofrece al sol el cadáver del tálamo
donde su hijo, cada noche,
se deja extraer por Dios
una costilla irrecuperable.
Dios exprime
la muerte en la sábana,
pero el cansancio de mi madre
le impide atisbar el milagro.
No la culpes, hombre de la cruz,
cuando reta al sol con humedad formidable.
Tú pendiste las horas como un ahorcado
y Dios exprimió tu sangre
desde su altura.
Tiende la sábana como gesto de rendición.
¿Ante quién flaquea mi madre cada semana?
¿Qué enemigo le obliga a retirarse
sin victorias que alimentar?
Dispongo a cerrar los ojos:
ya siento en mi vientre el cisma de Dios.
El almidón, justo padre,
maquilla silencioso una mortaja.

Saturday Shroud

When hanging out the sheets
like newly drowned bodies
an adjacent shirt
shrugs its shoulders.
The anointed one, no name worth remembering,
offers up to the sun a cadaver from the marriage bed
where her son, each night,
lets God extract
an irretrievable rib.
God wrings out
death over the sheet,
but my mother's tiredness
won't let her make out the miracle.
Don't blame her, man of the cross,
when she challenges the sun with a formidable dampness.
You strung the hours up like a hanged man
and God wrung out your blood
from on high.
She hangs the sheet out as a gesture of surrendering.
Who does my mother lose heart to each week?
What enemy forces her to retreat
no victories to nourish?
I'm ready to close my eyes:
now I feel the schism of God in my belly.
The starch, just father,
silently covers up a shroud.

Hierros de carnaval

Fraguados en herrerías clandestinas
viajan sobre *trailers* ominosos
por la cicatriz nacional,
artefactos para la diversión,
que en carnavales de barrio
se erigen en solo una hora.
Piezas de antiguos centrales
adobadas por años en el alcohol
de almíbar,
ahora toman sitio
en sillas voladoras y en
botes suspendidos en el arco
de su viaje.
Quien no asistió al esplendor
de los parques eléctricos,
podrá encontrar aquí
una desleal imitación.
Di adiós a tu hijo mientras
resiste su vértigo
en las pequeñas jaulas
de "El Exterminador".
Subamos a "El Dragón"
cuando su mal trazado ojo
ve derramar la cerveza sin nombre,
detenida en odres de extraño níquel
y disputada por caballeros de sed medieval.
Sobre las esteras de montaña rusa
oyendo crujir los frenos de la noria,
te dije: qué triste el país.
—Diviértete, fue la respuesta
mientras me alcanzabas un
algodón de azúcar,
traída del gran Brasil
en oscuras bodegas
de lujosos trasatlánticos.

Carnival Irons

Forged in clandestine smithies
they travel on ominous trailers
through the national scar,
artifacts for amusement,
in neighborhood carnivals
assembled in just an hour.
Pieces of old sugar mills
marinated for years in syrup
alcohol,
now they take their seats
in flying chairs and on
boats suspended in the arc
of their journey.
Those who never witnessed the splendor
of electric parks
will find here
an unfaithful imitation.
Say goodbye to your child while
he fights back his vertigo
in the small cages
of "The Exterminator."
Let's ride "The Dragon"
when its badly drawn eye
sees nameless beer spilled,
lingering in wineskins made of a strange nickel
and argued over by knights with a medieval thirst.
Standing on the roller coaster's carpet
hearing the brakes of the Ferris wheel grind
I told you: this country is so sad.
"Have fun," was the answer
while you got me some
cotton candy
brought from grand Brazil
in the dark holds
of luxury ocean liners.

Avenida del Puerto

Solo un tendón de grúa
pudo arrancar de un tajo
al framboyán sorprendido.
Por la Avenida del Puerto
es trasladado sobre la
espalda de un camión
—hijo del palimpsesto y la inventiva—
hacia su parterre de cemento,
sitio donde brindará sombra
cubana, al viajante de los cruceros.
Bien se sabe que uno de
diez logra resucitar al
prender sus venas
en la roca de petróleo.
Pero el Puerto de La Habana
merece ramilletes de púrpura
que hinchen más tarde
la postal y el obturador.
Si volviera de la muerte
el pintor Jay Matamoros
no hallaría en el repatriado
motivo para la estampa.
Su ojo naif solía detenerse
en la copa silvestre que amparaba
al guajiro en la tregua del mediodía,
lejos del salitre que ahora
empaña la flor de sangre.

Avenida del Puerto

Only the tendon of a crane
with just one slash could remove
the astonished flamboyant tree.
Down Avenida del Puerto
it's transported on
the back of a truck
—child of palimpsest and inventiveness—
toward its cement flower garden,
site where it will offer Cuban
shade to the cruise line traveler.
It's well known that one out of
ten manages to revive when
their veins take root
in the oil rock.
But Havana's Port
deserves bouquets of purple
later on swelling
postcard and shutter.
If the painter Jay Matamoros
were to come back from the dead
he'd find in his country
no motive for vignettes.
His primitivist eye would often linger
on the wild treetop sheltering
the peasant at the truce of midday,
far from the saltpeter that now
tarnishes the blood flower.

Jamila Medina Ríos (Holguin, 1981) is a poet, prose writer, essayist and editor. She won the coveted David Prize in 2009 with her first book of poetry and a collection of her essays received the prestigious Alejo Carpentier Prize in 2012. A book of short stories as well as another of poetry have appeared in Mexico. She was the Poetry Editor for Unión Publishers. She lives in Havana.

Langustia

Textos textos textos
tejeduras
lanzaderas
te (a)saltan sus gritos sobre la cabeza
te brotan de ella como pétalos
y de pronto: tienes toda la testa coronada
espinada de palabras

no es saludable (pare)ser un girasol
—dios no amanece
y húrtante el sitio de mirar
camino
desolado—
no es saludable la cabeza laureada
se deshoja después
como rama segada desde el invernadero
y los cristales que habían crecido en ella
quiébranse callados
apáganse: de velas
chisporrotean hacia dentro oh llama
demasiado arrimada al ventanal
abrupto
abierto

dejarse crecer la cabeza hacia dentro
—anahidrópica—
cierra todas las bocas que te hablan al oído
las venas muerdan(te)
huye de las compuertas los poros el encaje
cuida retrato de ti

si continuas dejando que te bailen
esos textos textos sobre la cabeza
que no te acabas de cortar
de hacer una sangría para extraer lo otro
si dejas se te prendan
ataduras al cuello

Ananguish

Texts texts texts
textures
shuttles
their cries (at)tack your skull
they spring from it like petals
and pronto: your entire head crowned
prickled with words

it's not healthy to (see)m a sunflower
—god doesn't dawn
and they swipe from you the looking spot
desolated
path—
it's not healthy a laureate head
later loses its leaves
like a cut branch from the greenhouse
and the crystals growing on it
silently break in two
snuffed: from candles
they spark toward the inside oh flame
too close to the picture window
abrupt
agape

to let your head grow toward the inside
—anahydropical—
closes all the mouths that speak in your ear
the veins bite(you)
flees the floodgates the pores the lace
cares for portrait of you

if you keep letting those texts texts
dance on your head
that you should cut off already
bloodletting to extract the other
if you let them tethers
take root in your neck

hilos que te indican pasadizos afuera (out of out of)
carne *haciafuerade* ti
si dejas que se aten cada uno a tu mano al pie
la mejilla (ofrecida):
repicarás en cien pedazos disgregado
—carnero
partícipe—
ojos colgando *carafuera*

es *lasfixia* lo que debes construir
hacia ti has de inclinar tu frente tuya
desdoblarte hacia ese espejo que has dejado empañar
enlutado (harto de barro)
la boca abierta la mirada
como lapa al cristal
—observante del otro—
ta(r)jas ta(r)jas ta(r)jas

taxidermia de ti
sembrarse un sitio y zambúllete en tu boca :
gargantabajo para siempre.

no quiero ver(te) burbujas
barbotear borbotear desde tu labio
desesperado hálito
nostálgico del otro
palabras sueltas que pretendan (ll)amar
—aludan—
referente
reflejo

respiradentro
tala tala tala
ten el pulcro civismo de presentar al aire:
una cabeza (por fin) descoronada.

threads pointing out passages out (afuera afuera)
flesh *towardtheoutsideof* you
if you let them tie each one to your hand foot
cheek (offered)
you'll toll in a hundred pieces scattered
–bellwether
participant–
eyes hanging *faceout*

it's *anasphyxiation* you should build
toward you you must bend your forehead your
unfold toward that mirror you've let fog up
mournful (stuffed with clay)
mouth open look
like a leech on the glass
–observer of the other–
(s)cores (s)cores (s)cores

taxidermy of you
sow a spot and plunge into your mouth :
throatdown for always.

i don't want to see(your) bubbles
murble burble from your lip
desperate breath
nostalgic for the other
words unleashed hoping to c(all)
–allude–
referent
reflex

breathinside
felling felling felling
have the meticulous civility to present to the air:
a head (at last) decrowned.

Palpo/ antena/ tentacularcio

Callada escruto en mí la música tranquila
que sobreviene al caos
al pataleo de los dedos succionados
por el rosa sediento.

En la humedad qué paz hallar
en lo sombrío en la tardanza en la víspera
del ciempiés de palpos
que abandona temblando el baptisterio
qué sequedad a que agarrarse qué oquedades
en que embutir la ventosa:
un (a)brazo que afinque para hociquear arriba
cuerpo por hombros apenas
mano callosa en columnata
y los muñones de las piernas
arribabajo
y atrás y alante columpiados sin brida.

Si no doy pie si no hallo a tientas el interruptor
el asidero: cuenco o co(r)no abierto a la lamida
si no amordazo las cabañas de la noche
o entierro dedos en el pelo...
no suelto prenda
no regurgito el salto.

Raspando con cuchara
el dienteperro
las yemas metidas en un agua de rosas
manos entrando al manadero
duro siglos

mas
cuando se recogen
los aperos del día
no quedo quieta en mí:

temiendo al daño
la lengua repta en las paredes del cerebro
buscando un dardo y una cerrazón

Palp/ Antenna/ Tentaculary

Silently I pour over the soothing music in me
that follows the chaos
the kicking of fingers suctioned
by the thirsty pink.

In dampness what peace can be found
in the dismal in the delay on the eve
of the centipede of palps
deserting the baptistery in trembles
what dryness to hold onto what hollows
to stuff the sucker in:
an em(brace) settling to root around above
body for shoulders scarcely
hand calloused in colonnade
and stumps for legs
updown
and backforth swung bridleless.

If I can't touch bottom if feeling my way I can't find the switch
the handle: bowl or cone(horn) open to licking
if I don't muzzle night's cabins
or bury fingers in hair
I don't let go
I don't regurgitate the leap.

Scraping the dogtooth
spar with a spoon
fingertips sunken in rosewater
hands entering the spring
I last centuries

yet
when the day's tools
are gathered
I don't stay still in me:

fearing the damage
tongue slithering on brain walls
searching for dart and closure

la escarbadura
el escondite en el otro
que agrieta el pecho
del que explora.

En esta gruta estuve ya
saqué los dedos encendidos
de la avispa del agua
y rosa flameaba el centro
y rosa flameaban las yemas
que se escondían de cabeza
en el manadero de tales.

Hay una lengua de deseo
que me trago cuando vienen los golpes
de la espuma
y el cuerpo cripta se levanta
como una araña una culebra
emasculada con un palo
un avispero de tierra.

Para verme callar para verme caer
han bajado los puentes giratorios.

Palpo-ícaro-antena
me estiro otra noche
buscándome las puntas de los pies
el centro de la espalda sin lavar
la ye(r)ma blanda del cráneo.

¿Se calmará el anemonario
atizado
por la aurora de casquivanos dedos
o habrá que sombrear las puntas
y estirar la palma
como Lady Lazarus
cortándolos caer?

Yo solo digo
por cada palpo
un tentáculo.

the unearthing
the hideout in the other
cracking the chest
of the explorer.

I was already in that grotto
pulled burning fingers
from the water wasp
and the center flamed pink
and the tips flamed pink
hiding headlong
in the spring of such things.

There is a tongue of desire
I swallow when blows
of foam come
and my body crypt rises
like a spider like a serpent
emasculated with a stick
an earth hornet's nest.

To see me fall silent to see me fall
the swing bridges lower.

Palp-icarus-antenna
I stretch out one more night
searching for the tips of my toes
the middle of my unwashed back
the soft waistland of my cranium.

Will the anemonarium settle down
stirred up
by the dawn of wanton fingers
or must I darken the tips
and stretch out the palm
like Lady Lazarus
cutting them to fall?

I just say
for each palp
a tentacle.

Fur(n)ia

El ejercicio de la escritura apostado fuera de la escritura y escindiéndola con el rabo del ojo. Una cisura practicada en una escritura que se insiste furnia.
Huecos de araña, huecos de nariz, boca, cuencas de ojos, oídos, vulva, vagina, bahía de bolsa, ombligo, ano. E incluso el descubrimiento de intersticios bajo la lengua, entre los dientes y la encía, debajo de la rodilla, encima del codo, en la jabonera de las clavículas, en los 16 arcos entre dedo y dedo de los pies, en las axilas, en el vacío de las manos juntas y de las manos echadas hacia atrás, en las comisuras, en las arrugas de la frente, en los labios agrietados, en el hedor de las patas de gallina, en la hendidura de la entrepierna, bajo el peso de las trenzas y los senos, en la nuca rendida, en la blandura del tobillo, en los valles y altozanos del vientre, en la morada debajo de las uñas, en los pliegues ilegibles de las palmas de las manos, en las furnias rajadas del nudillo. Mujer agujereada, mujer (alfombra) arrollada, mujer (paracaídas) plegadura.
Mujer ubre y odre y útero. Mujer embocadura de río. Máter. Materia. Madreperla sobre madrépora. Madre-del-verbo. Ave María. Damajuana. Un cuerpo que desea a otro que soba y orada. Lecho de arena y concha, para ser (des)h/ollado. Playa, puerto, embarcadero, varadero, abrevadero, aliviadero, bebedero de yeguas y de patos.
Huevo. Ovario. Canasto.
Mujer de mimbre, caña flexible, cáñamo, flauta dulce, espiga, lirio desmadejado. Mujer de estambre. Punta bordada de mujer.
El ejercicio de la escritura como un latigazo en la carne para abrir zanjas y liberar fluidos. Mujer orines, mujer sangre, mujer fécula, mujer leche. Avalancha riada. Arrollo murmullo. Espumarajo arcada. Balanceo de columpio mujer. Nanadora. Acunadora. Sanadora. Vaina.
El ejercicio no como la erección de un panóptico sino como una obturación, ensanchamiento de la dilatación del ser habitada, explorada, cavada, perforada, aserrada, rajada, acribillada, trepanada, traspasada, desabrochada, desvirgada, defenestrada, abierta. La mujer la porosa. La leporina, la li(e)bre, la leprada. Y el ejercicio como una amputación de lo que no tiene y sobra. Matadura del padre al excavar la raja. Matadura de la madre al ejercitar el equilibrio con las manos extendidas sobre el cordón umbilical, y saltar la cuerda, hacer pulsos, tobilleras y argollas de narigón, y jugar al ahorcado. Clava y clavadura. Encaje: con un ejercicio haciadentro y haciafuera de inserción y deserción. Furia y furnia.

F(u)or(y)amen

The exercise of writing posted outside writing split by the corner of your eye. An incision practiced in a writing insisting on foramen.
Spider holes, nostrils, mouth, eye sockets, ears, vulva, vagina, pocket bay, navel, anus. And even the discovery of interstices under tongue, between teeth and gum, under knee, over elbow, in collarbone's soap dish, in the 16 arches between each toe, in armpits, in the hollow of hands together and hands behind, in corners of the mouth, on forehead's wrinkles, on chapped lips, in the stench of crow's feet, in groin's fissure, under the weight of braids and breasts, in surrendered nape, in ankle's softness, in womb's valleys and hillocks, in the purple between nails, in the illegible folds of palms, in the cracked foramens of knuckle. Woman pit, woman (carpet) thrown, woman (parachute) folded.
Woman udder and bota and uterus. Woman river opening. Mater. Matter. Mother of pearl over madrepore. Mother-ofthe-word. Ave Maria. Demijohn.
A body desiring another that fondles and bores through. Bed of sand and shell, to be (de)h/o/allowed. Seashore, seaport, boatyard, drydock, wateringhole, spillway, birdbath for bears and geese.
Egg. Ovary. Basket.
Wicker woman, flexible reed, hemp, sweet flute, spike, weakened lily. Stamen woman. Embroidered edge of woman.
The exercise of writing like a whip on flesh to open ditches and free fluids. Woman urine, woman blood, woman starch, woman milk. Avalanche flood. Coil murmur. Froth arcade. Swing swaying woman. Lullabyer. Rocker. Healer. Sheath.
The exercise not like the erection of a panoptic but like a shutter, widening of the dilation of being inhabited, explored, dug, drilled, sawed, sliced, riddled, trepanned, run through, unfastened, deflowered, defenestrated, opened. Woman porous. Leporine, leveret, leprous. And the exercise as an amputation of what she doesn't have and is more than enough. Father sore as the gash is excavated. Mother sore as equilibrium is practiced with hands open wide on the umbilical cord, and jumping rope, making bracelets, anklets, and nose rings, and playing hangman. Nail and nailing. Lace: with an exercise inwards and outwards of insertion and desertion. Fury and foramen.

Una escritura que se insiste ensenada tiene una rabia una península confesa, oracular. El armadillo que se encueva, que se acoquina, que se aova, que se empolla, puede empezar a vomitar garras lenguas tentáculos pezuñas. Extremidades. Palpos, pulpos. Vecindades. Mano en la oscuridad. Arañazos hilos. Lengua anhelante. Imán. Hambrunas. La escritura vaso constrictor, la escritura contenida, la escritura conteniendo ser la escritura abrazo. La voz de sirena corporizada perfume, pañuelito al viento, valla de publicidad. Mujer brazo gitano. Mujer brazo, duro, de la ley. Magnolia de acero. Magdalena desleída en el té, que atrae poderosamente… recuerdos. Lágrimas de cocodrilo. Estalactitas. Casimbas ojo del invierno. Mujer tijera, cuchillada, estaca, pica hielos, dientes de peineta, de sierra y de león. Mujer pasamontañas. Armadillo en chino: como el animal engalanado para cruzar la cordillera. Mujer muralla. Mujer fusta de cobra. Aviborada. Mujer pócima. Una escritura que mata a la mujer alargando su veneno, si se deja crecer la lengua y se autosacia o penetra, como un ouroboros infernal. Hermafroditismo en el tacto. Una sensibilidad que se empoza y se amordaza con su propia tentación.

Saca tu lengua, mujer, de la carnada. Cierra la boca. Los negros no se ríen alto, las mujeres no se abren tanto para comer o bostezar. Tápate eso, cochina. Una escritura que se mira y cuyo clítoris crece de excitación verbal es de temer. La furia en furnia. Silenciada. No la furnia en furia. Llamamiento. Llamarada. Esa mujer anémona. Hágase una p/hiel líquida que apague a la ninfómana. Ábrase mujer linfa. Apurar el trago amargo, probar con la lengua una escritura sin muerte ni grito ni dolor. Sin hincar las rodillas… sobre granos de trigo. La letra con sangre entra. Déjate hacer. Dejarse hacer. Dejarse ser…

A writing insisting it's cove has a rage a confessed, oracular peninsula. The armadillo that hides in a cave, takes fright, becomes egg, broods, can start to vomit claws tongues tentacles hooves. Extremities. Palps, Octopuses. Neighborhoods. Hand in darkness. Scratches threads. Eager tongue. Magnet. Famines. Writing vessel constrictor, writing contained, writing containing to be writing embrace. Siren voice corporalized perfume, handkerchief in the wind, billboard. Woman jelly roll. Woman long arm of the law. Iron magnolia. Madeleine dissolved in tea, powerfully attracting...memories. Crocodile tears. Stalactites. beachwells winter eye. Woman scissor, slash, stake, icepick, teeth of comb, blade, and lion. Woman balaclava. Armadillo in Chinese: like animal adorned to cross the mountain range. Woman wall. Woman cobra whip. Vipered.

Woman potion. A writing that kills woman lengthening her venom, if she lets her tongue grow and self-quenches or penetrates, like an infernal ouroboros. Hermaphroditism in the touch. A sensibility that forms pools and is muzzled with its own temptation.

Remove your tongue, woman, from the bait. Shut your mouth. Blacks don't laugh out loud, Women don't open their mouths wide to eat or yawn. Cover it, dirty girl. A writing that looks at itself and whose clitoris grows with verbal excitation is frightening. Fury in foramen. Silenced. Not foramen in fury. Call. Flash. That woman anemone. Turn to liquid skin/spleen to put out the nymphomaniac. Open woman lymph. To hurry bitter pill, taste with tongue a writing deathless cryless painless. Not kneeling down upon the grains of wheat. Spare the rod spoil the child. Let yourself go. To let oneself go. To let oneself be.

MOISÉS MAYÁN FERNÁNDEZ

Moisés Mayán Fernández (Holguín, 1983) is a poet, prose writer, and editor. He has a degree in History from the University of Holguín and is a graduate of the Onelio Jorge Cardoso Center for Literary Education. He has published three books of poetry and has received numerous prizes for his work. He lives in Holguín.

El hombre estacionario

Los pájaros pierden rápidamente el miedo
y aprenden a posarse junto a los gatos de cemento.

Pájaros que no han visto nunca un bosque real
con abedules, cipreses y álamos.

Frágiles seres de ciudad. La noche los sorprende
en aleros de altos edificios,
bajo las chimeneas de las fábricas
o en esos árboles que crecen
próximos a transitadas autopistas.

Pero con los gatos de cemento
han comenzado a aparecer en algunos techos,
pájaros inmóviles, que soportan la lluvia y el invierno
en un gesto de canto demorado.
Y seguramente pronto veremos
cómo surgen en nuestros jardines los árboles de hierro.
Con ramas a prueba de huracanes.
(No podrán los enamorados
raspar sus nombres en la corteza).
¿Y los tristes pájaros que nunca han visto un bosque
con abedules, cipreses y álamos?
¿Los pájaros que crecieron
en nidos de filamentos metálicos?
¿Sus sueños de amanecer
en la rama olorosa de una acacia,
un árbol auténtico, un bosque que cerrándose en torno
proteja a sus polluelos?

Veo los pájaros posándose junto a los gatos de cemento
mientras emplazan frente a mí la estatua de un hombre.
El Hombre.
Sufro las ansias de rozar sus miembros de mármol.
Yo tampoco he visto nunca un bosque real,
los abedules, cipreses y álamos han sido desterrados
de mi mente.

Me estoy convirtiendo en un hombre estacionario.

The Stationary Man

Birds quickly lose their fear
and learn to perch alongside concrete cats.

Birds that have never seen a real forest
with firs, cypresses, or poplars.

Fragile city beings. Night surprises them
on the eaves of tall buildings,
beneath factory smokestacks,
or on those trees that grow
next to busy freeways.

Still along with the concrete cats
on some rooftops have begun to appear
motionless birds, putting up with rain and winter
a sign of lingering birdsong.
And soon we'll surely see
how iron trees show up in our yards.
With hurricane-proof branches.
(Couples no longer
to carve their names in the bark).
What of the sad birds that have never seen a forest
with firs, cypresses, or poplars?
The birds that grew up
in metallic filament nests?
Their dreams of waking
on the fragrant branch of an acacia,
an actual tree, a forest surrounding
to protect their chicks?

I see the birds perching alongside concrete cats
while the statue of a man is placed in front of me.
The Man.
I suffer from the longing to touch his marble members.
I too have never seen a real forest,
the firs, the cypresses, and the poplars have been banished
from my mind.

I'm turning into a stationary man.

Extraño animal, inocencia

Los niños, si pueden, crecen.
José Saramago

Llega el tiempo en que descubres tras el enrejado de tu pecho
la muerte del antiguo animal de la inocencia.
Y quedas inmerso en la desesperante blancura del día.
Sin fuerzas. Viendo alzarse los manicomios.
Como algas en un océano de luz. Y eres isla dentro de isla.
Privado de la gravedad de los navíos. De las hermosas criaturas
que en sus bodegas cruzan el Atlántico. Caballos árabes.
Galgos. Monos. Quetzales. Y aquel extraño animal
apresado en los confines de Bikaner. La inocencia.

No por anunciada la muerte sorprende menos. Perturba.
Violenta con sus derrumbes interiores la jaula/corazón.
Te asomas al enrejado y ves al animal inmóvil. Palideces.
Algo de ti parte con él. Se astilla contra los muñones
de la cárcel donde apresaste la inocencia.
Es el riesgo de volverse adulto. De crecer.
Desprendimientos. Quebraduras.
El ciclo humano. Estaciones que el brazo de Dios
va segando en el peligroso paisaje de la vida.
Perder la inocencia es adentrarse en los manicomios.
Asumir gota a gota el bebedizo del *delírium*.

Buscas señales de agresión. Dentelladas. Saetas.
El pozo de sangre fluyendo en la garganta.
Y no adviertes la rojez homicida de quien mata.
La marca de unos dedos entre el pelaje.
O un coágulo de dolor en los ojos. Muy abiertos.
Es natural la muerte de la inocencia. (*Natural & muerte*
son términos de compleja asociación —lo reconozco).
Ah, pobreza del idioma. Incapaz de precisar el martirio.
Agónicas noches del espécimen que se sabe
definido por la fatalidad. No antílope. Perro de aguas.
Pájaro de fuego. Sino un extraño animal
apresado en los confines de Bikanir. La inocencia.

Strange Animal, Innocence

Children, if they can, grow.
José Saramago

The time comes when you discover behind the latticework of your chest
the death of the old animal innocence.
And you linger immersed in day's exasperating whiteness.
Limp. Watching the insane asylums go up.
Like seaweed in an ocean of light. And you're the island within the island.
Deprived of vessel gravity. Of the beautiful creatures
who cross the Atlantic in their holds. Arabian horses.
Greyhounds. Monkeys. Quetzals. And that strange animal
captured in the confines of Bikaner. Innocence.

Though heralded death still surprises. Disrupts.
It forces open the cage/heart with its inner cave-ins.
You come to the latticework and see the motionless animal. You grow pale.
Something of you parts with it. It splinters against the stumps
of the prison where you captured innocence.
It's the hazard of becoming an adult. Of growing up.
Landslides. Fissures.
The human cycle. Seasons the arm of God
reaps in life's dangerous landscape.
To lose innocence is to go deep into asylums.
To take on *delirium's* potion drop by drop.

You search for signs of aggression. Tooth marks. Arrows.
The blood well flowing in the throat.
And you don't warn the murder redness of who's killing.
The mark of some fingers on fur.
Or a clot of pain in the eyes. Wide open.
The death of innocence is natural. (*Natural & death*
are terms with a complex association —I know).
Oh, poverty of language. Incapable of making martyrdom precise.
Agonal nights of the specimen that knows
it's defined by its fatality. Not antelope. Water dog.
Fire bird. But a strange animal
captured in the confines of Bikaner. Innocence.

Hay que aprender a despedirse.
De la metálica ligereza del velocípedo en los pasillos.
De la casa donde crecimos. Del miedo a la noche.
(Inmensa tras los pórticos). Del Día de Reyes.
Del abuelo y sus historias. De la abuela y sus dulces.
De las tardes de domingo. Despedirse.
Soltar amarras. Con la gravedad de los navíos.
Con la resignación de las hermosas criaturas
que en sus bodegas cruzan el Atlántico. Caballos árabes.
Galgos. Monos. Quetzales. *Aves del sol y de la sombra*.

Llega el tiempo en que descubres tras el enrejado de tu pecho
la muerte del antiguo animal de la inocencia.
Y quieres volver a las fotografías.
Al álbum de las primeras veces. Cuando la manzana
de casas era el mundo. Y te despertaba la música
de la lluvia en los techos de zinc. Y eras feliz.
Y el animal —apenas una cría. Como tú.
Jugueteaba en la planicie de un pecho sin barrotes.

Quieres volver. Pero es imposible.
No hay otros paraísos que los paraísos perdidos.

We must learn to say good-bye.
To the velocipede metallic lightness in hallways.
To the house where we grew up. To being scared of the dark.
(Immense behind the arcades). To Three Kings Day.
To Grandpa and his stories. To Grandma and her sweets.
To Sunday afternoons. Say good-bye.
Cut loose the moorings. With the gravity of vessels.
With the resignation of beautiful creatures
who cross the Atlantic in their holds. Arabian horses.
Greyhounds. Monkey. Quetzals. *Birds of sun and shadow.*

The time comes when you discover behind the latticework of your chest
the death of the old animal innocence.
And you want to go back to the pictures.
To the album of first times. When the houses
on the block were the world. And you woke up to the music
of the rain on zinc rooftops. And you were happy.
And the animal –just a baby. Like you.
Playing around in the flatlands of an unbarred chest.

You want to go back. But it's impossible.
There are no paradises other than lost paradises.

Prehistoria

hagamos el poema a imagen del hombre,
pero eterno.

Bajo la sombra irregular de los helechos el último hombre de Cro-Magnon se contempla. El espejo de un charco helado le devuelve su rostro, donde coinciden el animal y el humano incipiente. Rostro sin embargo poseedor de la belleza de una estirpe perdida. Rara belleza de los únicos.
El hombre de Cro-Magnon desea tener una hermosa voz para cantarle a la ausencia, pero solo consigue gemidos monocordes. La evolución lo ha privado del don del habla. No puede siquiera imaginar, que allí, frente aquel espejo de hielo, esté por surgir la poesía. El último hombre de Cro-Magnon contempla su desapacible imagen y piensa: "Ahora solo quedamos tú y yo".

Prehistory

let us make the poem in the image of man,
but eternal.

Beneath the uneven shadow of ferns the last Cro-Magnon man gazes at himself. The frozen puddle mirror throws back his face where animal and emerging human overlap. A face nevertheless possessing the beauty of a lost breed. Rare beauty of ones of a kind.
The Cro-Magnon man wants to have a pretty voice to sing to absence, but it only amounts to monochord groans. Evolution has deprived him of the gift of speech. There, facing the icy mirror, he can't even imagine that poetry will soon surface. The last Cro-Magnon man gazes at his unpleasant image and thinks: "Now it's just you and me."

Efecto Spielberg

Soy uno de esos cuerpos apilados por buldóceres después de la Segunda Guerra Mundial. Un joven párroco que murió de tifus en el campo de concentración de Dachau. Un médico rumano. Un profesor eslavo que estudiaba el discriminante de los polinomios cuadráticos. Una niña con un absurdo vestido rojo.

Spielberg Effect

I'm one of those bodies piled up by bulldozers after World War II. A young parish priest who died from typhus in Dachau's concentration camp. A Romanian doctor. A Slavic professor who studied the discriminant of quadratic polynomials. A young girl in an absurd red dress.

LEGNA RODRÍGUEZ IGLESIAS

Legna Rodríguez Iglesias (Camagüey, 1984) is a poet, prose writer, and playwright. She has four books of poetry, the latest being *Hilo+Hilo* (2015). She has received the Julio Cortázar Ibero-American Short Story Prize in 2011 and the Casa de Las Américas Prize in Theater in 2016. She lives in Miami.

99

no te voy a leer un poema de Ezra Pound me advierte mamá por teléfono
te voy a leer la última ley que salió este año que también es poesía y te
    gustará
saber que solo con el seguro social se pueden casar las personas y no hay
que esperar a ser residente solo hay que ser persona y querer casarse
para leerse uno al otro cuantos poemas de Ezra Pound tú quieras a la hora
que quieras y en la postura que elijas me advierte mamá por teléfono
solo con el seguro social se pueden casar las personas y no hay que esperar
a ser residente solo hay que ser persona y querer casarse para leerse uno
al otro cuantos poemas de Ezra Pound tú quieras a la hora que quieras
y en la postura que elijas me quedo repitiendo yo cotorra sujeta a cambios
no es para leer poemas y menos de Ezra Pound que me casaré contigo
    es para
que entres en mí a la hora que quieras y en el lugar que quieras y en la
    forma
que consideres y lo rompas todo y lo desacralices todo si quieres o si no
    quieres

99

i'm not going to read you a poem by Ezra Pound mom informs me on
     the phone
i'm going to read you the latest law to come out this year which is also
     poetry and you'll be happy
to know people can get married with just social security numbers now
     and not
have to wait to be a resident just be a person and want to get married
to read as many poems by Ezra Pound as you want to each other whenever
you want and in the position you choose mom informs me on the phone
people can get married with just social security numbers and not have
     to wait
to be a resident just a person and want to get married to read as many
     poems by Ezra Pound as you want to each other whenever you want
and in the position you choose i keep repeating a chatterbox subject to
     changes
it's not to read poems much less by Ezra Pound that i'll get married to
     you it's so
you'll enter me whenever you want and wherever you want and the way
you like and tear everything and make everything unholy if you want to
     or not

33

las pajas que me hago esperando a Godot huelen a jurel en salsa de tomate
sin tomate y sin aceite y sin albahaca y sin fuego lento y sin fuego alto
emocionalmente peores que las pajas a las dos de la mañana
con deseos de tocar el timbre de todas las puertas de mi edificio
y en cada puerta pedir un fósforo para encender la cocina
cada uno de los días de este año en que se conmemora mi treinta
    aniversario
mentiría si afirmara que las pajas de la espera son capaces de alegrarme
volverme una mujer con tomate y con aceite y con albahaca
y sin dudas con jureles en todas partes del cuerpo de la mente y del
    espíritu
mentiría si afirmara que al mover un dedo despacio rápido despacio
se me olvida lo que tengo que hacer en lo adelante
mentiría si mi espíritu supone que algún día
de este año sorprendente en que se conmemora algo ya dicho en otras
    líneas
Godot regresará siendo el mismo y siendo todo lo que yo necesitaba

33

the getting off i do waiting for Godot smells like mackerel in tomato sauce
without tomato or oil or basil or low flame or high flame
emotionally worse than getting off at two in the morning
wanting to ring the doorbells of all the doors in my building
and at each door to ask for a match to light the stove
each day of this year when my thirtieth birthday is observed
i'd lie if it would prove getting off while waiting can make me happy
turn me back into a woman with tomato and with oil and with basil
and certainly with mackerels everywhere in my body and mind and spirit
i'd lie if it would prove that by moving a finger slow fast slow
i'd forget what i have to do from now on
i'd lie if my spirit imagined one day
in this surprising year when something already said in other lines is observed
Godot returned being himself and being everything i needed

77

Dios mío me regalaste una lengua de puerco viva que se movía en la olla de cocción
eléctrica y me sacaba la lengua y me instaba a ladrarle y morderla y metérmela en la vagina
una lengua de puerco gorda y rosada como mi lengua que se movía igual que mi lengua
yo conozco el movimiento yo sé moverla igual y causar esa misma provocación la misma
felicidad Dios mío ese regalo me cayó del cielo me volvió loca me desquició lo peor
fue cuando se ablandó abandonando movilidad abandonándome yo la conduje ahí
a ese tiempo y a ese espacio de modorra su muerte duró media hora Dios mío
por qué es hermosa la muerte y por qué uno se deleita en ella si en realidad lo que quiere
es quedarse coleando viviendo para siempre sobre la faz de la tierra la faz de cualquier
país incluso los Estados Unidos de América un país que ya sabemos que es sinónimo
de olla pues ya saqué mi cuchillo y saqué mi tenedor y ya me comí la lengua y ahora voy
a acostarme y a dormir profundamente y voy a soñar contigo moviéndote en la olla

my God you gave me a live pig's tongue that quivered in the electric
   cooker and it stuck its tongue out at me spurred me to bark at it and
   bite it and stick it up my vagina
a pig's tongue plump and pink like my tongue quivering just like my
   tongue i know that quiver i know how to move it just like that and
   cause the same
provocation the same happiness my God that gift fell straight out of
   heaven drove me crazy made me go off the deep end the worst
was when it softened leaving mobility behind leaving me behind i led it
   there
at that time and space of drowsiness its death lasted half an hour my God
   why is death beautiful and why do we delight in it if all it actually
   wants
is to keep on wagging its tail living for always on the face of the earth the
   face of any country even the United States of America a country we
   already know is a synonym
for cooker so i got out my knife and i got out my fork and i ate the tongue
   and now i'm
going to go to bed to sleep hard and i'll dream of you quivering in the
   cooker

11

mi alma está llena de metáforas adquiridas de generación en generación
mi alma está llena de símiles más o menos fascinantes que dan fe del agrado que hay en mí
mi alma posee un gran hipérbaton enquistado a la derecha que mide varios milímetros
y a su izquierda igualmente enquistada una onomatopeya palpable excedida
mi alma tiene una hipérbole relacionada con la necesidad de afecto femenino y masculino
esta mañana decidí hacer una obra de caridad a mi alma y recogí un saco de la basura
lleno de hermosos libros usados sobre ciencias agrónomas veterinarias y matemáticas
el oxímoron y la paradoja figuras lógicas de mi alma aumentaron sus latencias
nada se compara a esta felicidad que para no cansarlos experimento
ver mi alma desde afuera llena de esos síntomas que me mantienen joven
figuras de diálogo y patéticas figuras dialécticas y de ficción
todo en uno como esos paquetes de pequeños jabones de olor
que tanto agradan a las familias de más de seis integrantes

11

my soul's full of metaphors acquired from generation after generation
my soul's full of more or less fascinating similes that witness the kindness
    in me
my soul possesses a great hyperbaton encysted on the right side measuring
    various millimeters
and on the left likewise encysted a palpable excessive onomatopoeia
my soul has a hyperbole related to the need for feminine and masculine
    affect
this morning i decided to do charity work for my soul and i took
    out a garbage bag full of beautiful used books on the agronomic
    veterinarian and mathematical sciences
the oxymoron and the paradox logical figures in my soul increased their
    throbbing
nothing compares to this happiness that to not bore you i experience
when i see my soul from the outside full of these symptoms that keep
    me young
figures of dialogue and pathetic dialectical fictional figures
all-in-one like those packages of small bars of scented soap
that so please families with six members or more

66

haitiano varón durmiendo solo afuera frente a un frente frío es solo un tipo de asfixia
haitiano que ladra y muerde durmiendo solo afuera de cansancio de dolor de mordeduras
hombre que no interesa por haitiano por desnudo por hermoso por extraño y pobre
hombre mío para mí no me ladres no me muerdas que yo te voy a coser te voy a matar
el miedo añadiéndole mi miedo haitiano trabajador durmiendo solo afuera de su centro
de trabajo un edificio importante menos alto que un baobab menos maravilloso dónde
tu vives haitiano yo vivo aquí dónde tu naciste haitiano yo nací aquí dónde tú orinas
haitiano yo orino aquí yo como aquí yo amo aquí es solo un tipo de asfixia no intentes
quitarme el miedo porque yo no tengo miedo yo tengo un tesoro que no le he mostrado
a nadie y a ti tampoco te lo mostraré lo tengo por todo el cuerpo incluidos mis testículos
mi glande y mi prepucio es un tesoro que Dios me dio un tesoro haitiano llamado odio

66

haitian man sleeping alone outside facing a cold front is just one kind of suffocation
haitian who barks and bites sleeping alone outside from exhaustion from pain from bites
man of no interest because haitian because naked because beautiful because strange and poor
man mine for me don't bark at me don't bite me because i will sew you i will kill you
fear adding my fear haitian worker sleeping alone outside his place
of work an important building not as tall as a baobab not as marvelous where
do you live haitian i live here where were you born haitian i was born here where do you piss
haitian i piss here i eat here i love here it's just one kind of suffocation don't try
to take away my fear because i'm not afraid i have a treasure i haven't shown
to anyone you either i'll show you it's all over my body even my testicles
my glans and my foreskin it's a treasure God gave me a treasure haitian called hate

22

derecho al fondo más al fondo está eso que late y duele sin detenerse dios me libre
eso que ladra y muerde como un animal salvaje o como un pajarraco indígena en cautiverio
es el corazón en su concepto de alma lo más imbécil que uno tiene por delante
aquello que hace trizas lo que le rodea como el pensamiento y el discernimiento
convertidos en jugos biliares y echados hacia fuera a través de un órgano con muela
un órgano encargado de transmitir aquello que le dicta la conciencia o el alma
el párrafo anterior me lo ha dictado la conciencia o el alma a esta hora no sabría cuál
me he despertado y he venido derecho al fondo y he tecleado esto avergonzada
soñé con la palabra *ébola* y con la palabra *dengue* las vi en sueños las acaricié
el hombre que sueña con palabras ha llegado sin dudas a una edad en la que no hay tiempo
que perder y la mujer que sueña con palabras debe interpretar sus palabras de la manera
correcta o perderá su tiempo y sus palabras derecho al fondo está eso que te hace
perder el tiempo o ganarlo yo no perderé mis palabras aunque las interprete mal

22

straight back more toward the back is this beating and hurting non-stop god forbid
this beating and biting like a wild animal or like a big native bird captive
it's the heart in its concept of soul the most imbecilic we have ahead of us
what shatters what surrounds us like thought and discernment
changed to bile and tossed outside through an organ with molar
an organ entrusted with broadcasting what conscience or soul dictates
the previous paragraph has been dictated to me by conscience or soul right now i wouldn't know which
i've woken up and headed straight back and embarrassingly i've typed this
i dreamt of the word *ebola* of the word *dengue* i saw them in dreams i caressed them
the man who dreams of words has gotten no doubt to an age where there's no time
to waste and the woman who dreams of words must interpret her words in the right way
or waste her time and her words straight back is this making you
waste time or save it i won't waste my words even though i misunderstand them

SERGIO GARCÍA ZAMORA

Sergio García Zamora (Esperanza, 1986) is a poet, literary critic, and editor. He graduated from the Central University of Las Villas in Philology. He has published eleven books of prize-winning poetry. Most recently, the Fundación Loewe awarded him their prestigious Young Poet's Prize (2016).

La madre

mi madre se enternece oyendo un xilófono. según el diccionario: instrumento musical de percusión, hecho de tablillas de madera. el xilófono, no mi madre. pero si mi madre quiere se vuelve un instrumento, se vuelve musical, se vuelve de percusión, se arranca una tablilla y me da una zurra que me enternece. todo está en proponérselo como el padre de Beethoven, que no debió ser tan malo cuando el hijo fue tan bueno. lo de Beethoven era el piano; lo de su padre, la educación musical. un xilófono parece un piano. el xilófono, no mi madre. pero si mi madre quiere se vuelve toda piano y me deja caer sobre los dedos la tapa del teclado para que ande piano, para que nunca me recupere del enternecimiento, como lo haría el padre de Beethoven. o acaso mejor: como lo hace la madre del poeta.

Mother

my mother goes soft listening to a xylophone. according to the dictionary: musical instrument in the percussion family, made of wooden bars. the xylophone, not my mother. but if my mother wants to she turns into an instrument, she turns musical, she turns percussive, she pulls off a bar and gives me a beating that makes me go soft. it's all about suggesting it like Beethoven's father, who couldn't have been that bad when the son was so good. Beethoven's thing was the piano; his father's, musical education. a xylophone looks like a piano. the xylophone, not my mother. but if my mother wants to she turns into a piano and she lets the lid fall on my fingers so i'm piano, so i'll never be able to come back from going soft, like Beethoven's father would do it. or even better. like the poet's mother does.

Una casa sin ático

I

Amor mío, piensa en las ventajas de vivir en una casa sin ático: jamás vas a caerte al subir la escalerilla; ni van a caerse los niños que gustan de jugar allí; ni tendrás que limpiarlo, aunque sea apenas una vez al año. Imagina el horror de descubrir algunas ratas. No creo que logres soportarlo. Además, de ningún modo las familias se deshacen de las cosas inútiles, solo las dejan en el ático. Un ático nunca sirve para nada, salvo para guardar cadáveres: juguetes rotos, santos de madera, el árbol con los adornos navideños. Cadáveres de la infancia perdida, de la fe perdida, de la felicidad perdida. Y fotos, cientos de fotos en cajas de zapatos.

II

Me encierro en el ático de una casa sin ático. Me encierro a escribir de la vida escondido de la vida. Si preguntan, dirás que salí a caminar un rato. Una excusa verosímil que los amigos perdonan. Una excusa verdadera. Prefiero pasear en invierno para no encontrar a más de dos o tres conocidos. Nada personal. Lo mejor de los misántropos es que nunca celebrarán un congreso. Lo mejor de los misántropos es que saben reconocerse como un asesino reconoce a otro asesino en esas mesas de un café cualquiera. Si preguntan, dirás que salí a caminar conmigo. Me encierro a escribir. Me encierro a escribir. Me encierro. Qué frío hace en el ático de una casa sin ático.

III

Peor que una casa sin ático es un país sin ático. ¿Dónde queda el ático de un país? ¿En su montaña más alta? ¿En su mente más lúcida? ¿En su mejor líder, en su mejor héroe, en su mejor poeta? ¿O en su hijo más inocente? Desempolvar el ático del país. Atisbar por su ojo de buey la tormenta que se avecina. Peor que una casa sin ático es un país sin ático: un país hecho de sótanos.

A House with No Attic

I

My love, think of the advantages of living in a house with no attic: you'll never fall from the ladder, the children who like to play there won't either, you won't have to clean it, even if it's just once a year. Think of the horror of discovering rats. I don't think you could handle it. Besides, there's no way families get rid of useless things, they just leave them in the attic. An attic is useless, except for hanging on to cadavers: broken toys, wooden saints, the tree with Christmas decorations. Cadavers from lost childhood, lost faith, lost happiness. And photos, hundreds of photos in shoe boxes.

II

I lock myself away in the attic of a house with no attic. I lock myself away to write of life hidden from life. If they ask, tell them I've gone on a little walk. A verisimilar excuse friends will forgive. A real excuse. I prefer to stroll in winter so I only meet up with two or three people I know. Nothing personal. The best thing about misanthropes is that they'll never hold a conference. The best thing about misanthropes is that they recognize one another like a murderer recognizes another murderer at those tables in some café. If they ask, tell them I've gone on a little walk with myself. I lock myself away to write. I lock myself away to write. I lock myself away. It's so cold in the attic of a house with no attic.

III

Worse than a house with no attic is a country with no attic. Where's a country's attic? On the highest mountain? In its most lucid mind? In its best leader, its best hero, its best poet? Or its most innocent child? To dust off the country's attic. To keep an eye on the approaching storm through its porthole. Worse than a house with no attic is a country with no attic: a country of basements.

El camionero y yo

la primera vez que escuché un poema, un poema de Charles Bukowski, fue en la cabina de un camión. era un programa radial y el camionero subió el volumen. en cualquier momento, pensé, apaga la radio esta bestia. pero el camionero siguió escuchando. lo de Bukowski no tenía nombre: hablaba con cierto orgullo sobre las borracheras de su padre y sobre las golpizas de su padre. parecía decir que a él, Charles Bukowski, ni borracheras ni golpizas lo habían logrado arruinar. después pusieron música y el camionero se colocó sus gafas. estos programas de radio, gruñó, nunca sirven para nada. la primera vez que escuché un poema, un poema de Charles Bukowski, fue mientras viajaba a casa. un camionero nos puede engañar.

The Truck Driver and Me

the first time i heard a poem, a poem by Charles Bukowski, was in the cab of a truck. it was a radio program and the truck driver turned up the volume. i thought, this jerk is going to turn off the radio any second. but the truck driver kept listening. the Bukowski thing was incredible: he spoke somewhat proudly about his father getting drunk and beating him. it seemed like what he was saying was that drunken bouts and beatings hadn't been able to ruin him, Charles Bukowski. later on they played music and the truck driver put on his sunglasses. these radio programs, he growled, are pointless. the first time i heard a poem, a poem by Charles Bukowski, was when i was going home. sometimes a truck driver can fool us.

Poemas con neblina

poemas con neblina, horrendos poemas con neblina donde nunca se logra conducir, si no es a riesgo de estrellarse. los nuevos poetas neblinosos gustan de nombrar a Londres sin haber ido a Londres, como si la neblina fuese privativa de esa ciudad, como si no hubiese neblina en otros países, en otras ciudades que conquistó Inglaterra. poemas con neblina, horrendos poemas con neblina donde las luces del auto descubren tu doble fantasmal. los nuevos poetas neblinosos gustan de tenderse sobre la hierba como un cuerpo más bajo la neblina, a riesgo de agarrar el Gran Resfrío y morirse sin ver Londres, sin ver otra ciudad ni otro país espléndido como Inglaterra. poemas con neblina, horrendos poemas con neblina que me hacen recordar a mi abuelo: hoy habrá un sol tremendo.

Poems with Fog

poems with fog, horrendous poems with fog where you can't drive unless you risk crashing into something. the new foggy poets like to name London without having gone to London, as if fog were exclusive to that city, as if there wasn't fog in other countries, in other cities conquered by England. poems with fog, horrendous poems with fog where car lights uncover your ghostly double. the new foggy poets like to stretch out on the grass like just another body beneath the fog, risking the Great Cold and dying without seeing London, without seeing another city or splendid country like England. poems with fog, horrendous poems with fog that make me think of my grandfather: today will be bright and sunny.

Balada para colgarse

a François Villón, el maldito, lo suben y lo bajan de la horca un poeta después de otro. no fui a la universidad, dice Villón, para ser un pelele; no gané el favor del rey, para ser un muñeco de paja. un poeta después de otro lo piden para sus bandas; todos quieren a ese francés en sus cochinas bandas, a ese diablo criado por un monje. el maldito de François se ríe: piensa deshacerse del cabecilla y tomar el mando. entre poetas también se está entre putas y ladrones. a François Villón, el maldito, lo suben y lo bajan de la horca un poeta después de otro. no escribí para esto, dice Villón, no robé ni maté para esto. si quieren entonar mi balada, pónganse la soga al cuello.

Ballad for Hanging Oneself

François Villón, that devil, one poet after another sends him to and lowers him from the gallows. i didn't go to college, Villón says, to be a pushover; didn't win the king's favor to be a straw man. one poet after another wants him for their gang; they all want that Frenchman in their stinking gangs, that rogue raised by a priest. that devil François laughs: thinks about getting rid of the ringleader and taking over. even among poets you're among whores and thieves. François Villón, that devil, one poet after another sends him to and lowers him from the gallows. this isn't why i wrote, Villón says, this isn't why i stole and killed. if you want to sing my ballad, put the rope round your own neck.

Acknowledgements

Earlier versions of the introduction and many of these poems in translation appeared in *Kenyon Review* (XL. 1. Jan/Feb 2018) and *The Wolf* (35).

The epigraph from "Café Bulevar Effect" comes from *Complete Poetry of Osip Emilevich Mandelstam*. Translation by Burton Raffel and Alla Burago. Albany: SUNY Press, 1973. 119.

The epigraph from "The Death of Objects" is taken from *Tractatus Logico-Philosophicus*. Translation by C.K. Ogden. New York: Routledge, 1990. 35.

Editors / Translators:

KATHERINE M. HEDEEN is specialist in Latin American po and has both written extensi on and translated contempo authors from the region. translations include collections Rodolfo Alonso, Juan Bañue Juan Calzadilla, Juan Gel Fayad Jamís, Hugo Mujica, J Emilio Pacheco, Víctor Rodríg Núñez, and Ida Vitale, among m others. She is the Poetry Transla Editor for the Kenyon Rev and a two-time recipient of a NEA Translation Project Grant. resides in Ohio where she is Professor of Spanish at Kenyon Coll

VÍCTOR RODRÍGUEZ NÚÑ (Havana, 1955) is one of Cu most outstanding and celebra contemporary writers. Over collections of his poetry ap throughout Latin America Europe, and he has been recipient of major awards all the Spanish-speaking wo including, in 2015, the cov Loewe Prize, the highest hono unpublished book of poetry can receive in the region. He has compiled t anthologies that define his poetic generation, as well as another of 20th cen Cuban poetry, *La poesía del siglo XX en Cuba* (2011). He has brought out vari critical editions, introductions, and essays on Spanish American poets. divides his time between Gambier, Ohio, where he is currently Professo Spanish at Kenyon College, and Havana, Cuba.

El vuelo (Estudio para una ilustración publicada en El Caimán Barbudo), / The Flight (Study for an Illustration Published in El Caimán Barbudo), 1982

The original art used for the cover design of this volume, seen above in its original version, was generously provided by Tonel. (Cover design and typography is by Elae / Lynne DeSilva-Johnson)

TONEL (Antonio Eligio Fernández, Havana, 1958) is an artist, critic, curator and educator. A graduate of University of Havana in Art History (1982), he has exhibited extensively, including at the Havana, Sao Paulo, Berlin, and Venice biennials. He has most recently shown his work at a solo exhibition *Ajústate al tema*, which opened in December 2018 at the Museo Nacional de Bellas Artes, Havana, Cuba. Since 2006 he has taught as an adjunct professor and a sessional lecturer at the Department of Art History, Visual Art and Theory, University of British Columbia, Vancouver, Canada. He is currently a visiting artist and scholar at the Latin American Studies Center at Stanford University.

RECENT & FORTHCOMING FULL LENGTH
OS PRINT::DOCUMENTS and PROJECTS,
2018-19

2019

Y - Lori Anderson Moseman
Ark Hive-Marthe Reed
I Made for You a New Machine and All it Does is Hope - Richard Lucyshyn
Illusory Borders-Heidi Reszies
A Year of Misreading the Wildcats - Orchid Tierney
We Are Never The Victims - Timothy DuWhite
Of Color: Poets' Ways of Making | An Anthology of Essays on Transformative Poetics - Amanda Galvan Huynh & Luisa A. Igloria, Editors
The Suitcase Tree - Filip Marinovich
In Corpore Sano: Creative Practice and the Challenged* Body - Elae [Lynne DeSilva-Johnson] and Amanda Glassman, Editors

KIN(D)* TEXTS AND PROJECTS

A Bony Framework for the Tangible Universe-D. Allen
Opera on TV-James Brunton
Hall of Waters-Berry Grass
Transitional Object-Adrian Silbernagel

GLOSSARIUM: UNSILENCED TEXTS AND TRANSLATIONS

Śnienie / Dreaming - Marta Zelwan, (Poland, trans. Victoria Miluch)
Alparegho: Pareil-À-Rien / Alparegho, Like Nothing Else - Hélène Sanguinetti (France, trans. Ann Cefola)
High Tide Of The Eyes - Bijan Elahi (Farsi-English/dual-language) trans. Rebecca Ruth Gould and Kayvan Tahmasebian
In the Drying Shed of Souls: Poetry from Cuba's Generation Zero Katherine Hedeen and Víctor Rodríguez Núñez, translators/editors
Street Gloss - Brent Armendinger with translations for Alejandro Méndez, Mercedes Roffé, Fabián Casas, Diana Bellessi, and Néstor Perlongher (Argentina)
Operation on a Malignant Body - Sergio Loo (Mexico, trans. Will Stockton)
Are There Copper Pipes in Heaven - Katrin Ottarsdóttir (Faroe Islands, trans. Matthew Landrum)

2018

An Absence So Great and Spontaneous It Is Evidence of Light - Anne Gorrick
The Book of Everyday Instruction - Chloë Bass
Executive Orders Vol. II - a collaboration with the Organism for Poetic Research
One More Revolution - Andrea Mazzariello
Chlorosis - Michael Flatt and Derrick Mund
Sussuros a Mi Padre - Erick Sáenz
Abandoners - Lesley Ann Wheeler
Jazzercise is a Language - Gabriel Ojeda-Sague
Born Again - Ivy Johnson
Attendance - Rocío Carlos and Rachel McLeod Kaminer
Singing for Nothing - Wally Swist
Walking Away From Explosions in Slow Motion - Gregory Crosby
Field Guide to Autobiography - Melissa Eleftherion

KIN(D)* TEXTS AND PROJECTS

Sharing Plastic - Blake Neme
The Ways of the Monster - Jay Besemer

GLOSSARIUM: UNSILENCED TEXTS AND TRANSLATIONS

The Book of Sounds - Mehdi Navid (Farsi dual language, trans. Tina Rahimi
say: The Flame of the Jungle - María Vázquez Valdez (Mexico, trans. Margaret Randall)
urn Trip / Viaje Al Regreso - Israel Dominguez; (Cuba, trans. Margaret Randall)

for our full catalog please visit:
https://squareup.com/store/the-operating-system/

deeply discounted Book of the Month and Chapbook Series subscriptions
are a great way to support the OS's projects and publications!
sign up at: http://www.theoperatingsystem.org/subscribe-join/

GLOSSARIUM : UNSILENCED TEXTS

The Operating System's GLOSSARIUM: UNSILENCED TEXTS series was established in early 2016 in an effort to recover silenced voices outside and beyond the canon, seeking out and publishing both contemporary translations and little or un-known out of print texts, in particular those under siege by restrictive regimes and silencing practices in their home (or adoptive) countries. We are committed to producing dual-language versions whenever possible.

Few, even avid readers, are aware of the startling statistic reporting that less than three percent of all books published in the United States, per UNESCO, are works in translation. Less than one percent of these (closer to 0.7%) are works of poetry and fiction. You can imagine that even less of these are experiemental or radical works, in particular those from countries in conflict with the US or where funding is hard to come by.

Other countries are far, far ahead of us in reading and promoting international literature, a trend we should be both aware of and concerned about—how does it come to pass that our attentions become so myopic, and as a result, so under-informed? We see the publication of translations, especially in volume, to be a vital and necessary act for all publishers to require of themselves in the service of a more humane, globally aware, world. By publishing 7 titles in 2019, we stand to raise the number of translated books of literature published in the US this year *by a full percent*. We plan to continue this growth as much as possible.

The dual-language titles either in active circulation or forthcoming in this series include Arabic-English, Farsi-English, Polish-English, French-English, Faroese-English, Yaqui Indigenous American translations, and Spanish-English translations from Cuba, Argentina, Mexico, Uruguay, Bolivia, and Puerto Rico.

The term 'Glossarium' derives from latin/greek and is defined as 'a collection of glosses or explanations of words, especially of words not in general use, as those of a dialect, locality or an art or science, or of particular words used by an old or a foreign author.' The series is curated by OS Founder and Managing Editor Elæ [Lynne DeSilva-Johnson,] with the help of global collaborators and friends.

WHY PRINT / DOCUMENT?

The Operating System uses the language "print document" to differentiate from the book-object as part of our mission to distinguish the act of documentation-in-book-FORM from the act of publishing as a backwards-facing replication of the book's agentive *role* as it may have appeared the last several centuries of its history. Ultimately, I approach the book as TECHNOLOGY: one of a variety of printed documents (in this case, bound) that humans have invented and in turn used to archive and disseminate ideas, beliefs, stories, and other evidence of production.

Ownership and use of printing presses and access to (or restriction of printed materials) has long been a site of struggle, related in many ways to revolutionary activity and the fight for civil rights and free speech all over the world. While (in many countries) the contemporary quotidian landscape has indeed drastically shifted in its access to platforms for sharing information and in the widespread ability to "publish" digitally, even with extremely limited resources, the importance of publication on physical media has not diminished. In fact, this may be the most critical time in recent history for activist groups, artists, and others to insist upon learning, establishing, and encouraging personal and community documentation practices. Hear me out.

With The OS's print endeavors I wanted to open up a conversation about this: the ultimately radical, transgressive act of creating PRINT /DOCUMENTATION in the digital age. It's a question of the archive, and of history: who gets to tell the story, and what evidence of our life, our behaviors, our experiences are we leaving behind? We can know little to nothing about the future into which we're leaving an unprecedentedly digital document trail — but we can be assured that publications, government agencies, museums, schools, and other institutional powers that be will continue to leave BOTH a digital and print version of their production for the official record. Will we?

As a (rogue) anthropologist and long time academic, I can easily pull up many accounts about how lives, behaviors, experiences — how THE STORY of a time or place — was pieced together using the deep study of correspondence, notebooks, and other physical documents which are no longer the norm in many lives and practices. As we move our creative behaviors towards digital note taking, and even audio and video, what can we predict about future technology that is in any way assuring that our stories will be accurately told – or told at all? How will we leave these things for the record?

In these documents we say:
WE WERE HERE, WE EXISTED, WE HAVE A DIFFERENT STORY

- Elæ [Lynne DeSilva-Johnson], Founder/Creative Director
THE OPERATING SYSTEM, Brooklyn NY 2018

DOC U MENT
/däkyəmənt/

First meant "instruction" or "evidence," whether written or not.

noun - a piece of written, printed, or electronic matter that provides information or evidence or that serves as an official record
verb - record (something) in written, photographic, or other form
synonyms - paper - deed - record - writing - act - instrument

[*Middle English, precept, from Old French, from Latin documentum, example, proof, from docre, to teach; see dek- in Indo-European roots.*]

Who is responsible for the manufacture of value?

Based on what supercilious ontology have we landed in a space where we vie against other creative people in vain pursuit of the fleeting credibilities of the scarcity economy, rather than freely collaborating and sharing openly with each other in ecstatic celebration of MAKING?

While we understand and acknowledge the economic pressures and fear-mongering that threatens to dominate and crush the creative impulse, we also believe that ***now more than ever we have the tools to relinquish agency via cooperative means,*** fueled by the fires of the Open Source Movement.

Looking out across the invisible vistas of that rhizomatic parallel country we can begin to see our community beyond constraints, in the place where intention meets resilient, proactive, collaborative organization.

Here is a document born of that belief, sown purely of imagination and will.
When we document we assert.
We print to make real, to reify our being there.

When we do so with mindful intention to address our process, to open our work to others, to create beauty in words in space, to respect and acknowledge the strength of the page we now hold physical, a thing in our hand, we remind ourselves that, like Dorothy:
we had the power all along, my dears.

THE PRINT! DOCUMENT SERIES
is a project of
the trouble with bartleby
in collaboration with
the operating system

www.ingramcontent.com/pod-product-compliance
Lightning Source LLC
Chambersburg PA
CBHW030114100526
44591CB00009B/401